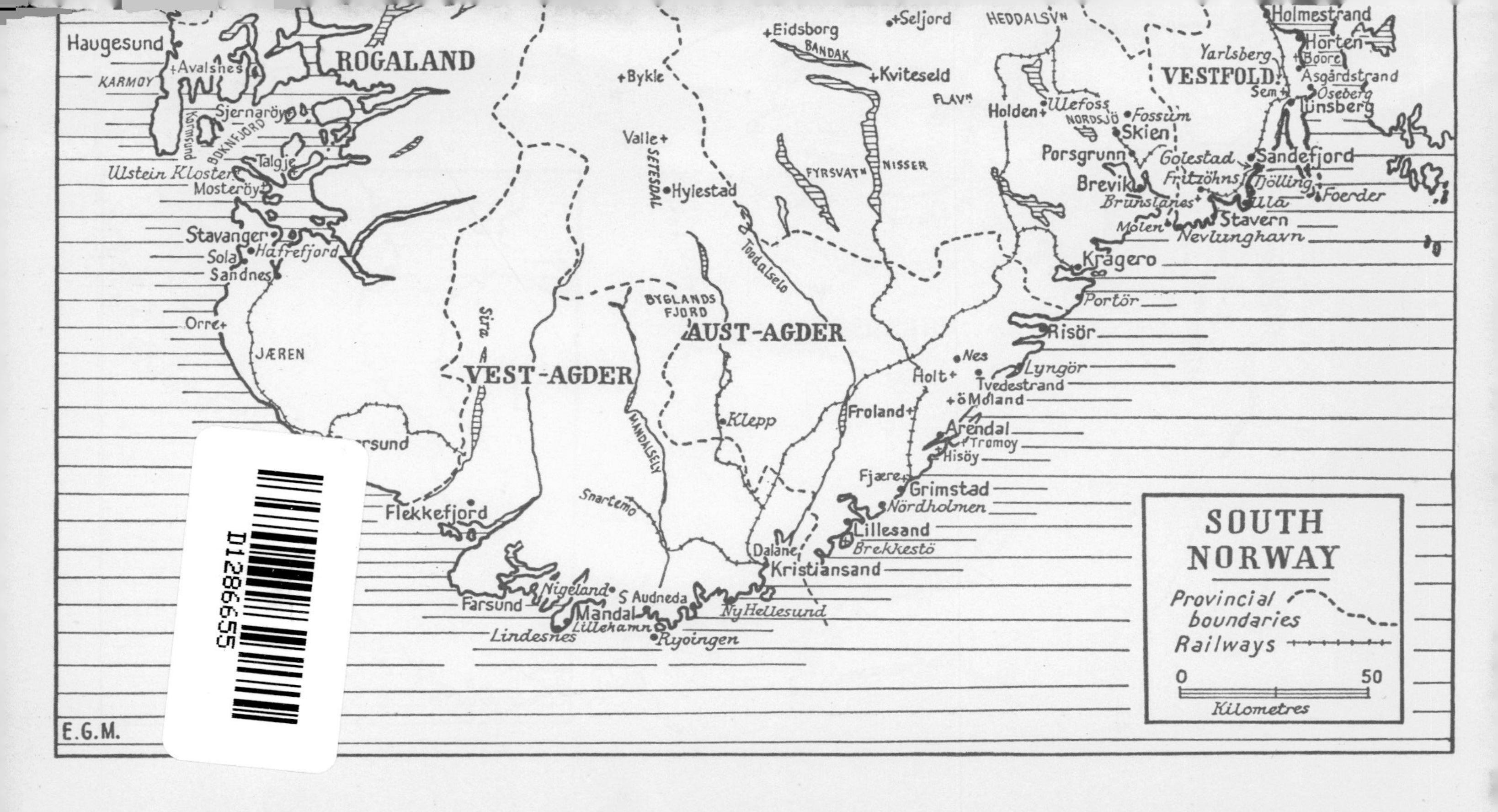

SOUTH NORWAY
Provincial boundaries
Railways
0
50
Kilometres
ROGALAND
VEST-AGDER
AUST-AGDER
VESTFOLD
Haugesund
KARMOY
Avalsnes
Karmsund
Sjernaröy
BOKNFJORD
Talgje
Ulstein Kloster
Mosteröy
Stavanger
Sola
Hafrefjord
Sandnes
Orre
JÆREN
Sira
Flekkefjord
Farsund
Lindesnes
Nigeland
Mandal
Lillehamn
S Audneda
Ryoingen
Ny Hellesund
Snartemo
MANDALSELV
Dalane
Kristiansand
Brekkestö
Lillesand
Nördholmen
Grimstad
Fjære
Hisöy
Tromoy
Arendal
Moland
Tvedestrand
Lyngör
Nes
Holt
Froland
Klepp
BYGLANDS FJORD
Toodalselo
Hylestad
SETESDAL
Valle
Bykle
Eidsborg
BANDAK
Kviteseld
Seljord
FYRSVATN
NISSER
FLAVN
HEDDALSVN
Holden
Ulefoss
NORDSJÖ
Fossum
Skien
Porsgrunn
Brevik
Brunslanes
Golestad
Fritzöhns
Sandefjord
Tjölling
Ula
Foerder
Mølen
Stavern
Nevlunghavn
Kragero
Portör
Risör
Yarlsberg
Holmestrand
Horten
Boore
Asgårdstrand
Oseberg
Sem
Tunsberg
E.G.M.

SOUTH NORWAY

by the same author

NORTH NORWAY

THE HEART OF NORWAY

WEST NORWAY

EAST NORWAY

1. Processional dragon's head from Oseberg

SOUTH NORWAY

FRANK NOEL STAGG

FOREWORD BY
PROFESSOR
Alf Sommerfelt
D. ès L., D.Litt. (Oxon), LL.D. (Glasgow), D.Litt. Celt. (Dubl.)

Ruskin House
GEORGE ALLEN & UNWIN LTD
MUSEUM STREET LONDON

FIRST PUBLISHED IN 1958

PRINTED IN GREAT BRITAIN
in 12 pt Fournier type
BY THE WHITEFRIARS PRESS LTD
LONDON AND TONBRIDGE

Dedicated
to the People of Norway
with the author's
affection and admiration

INTRODUCTION

This is the last of the original and interesting books which Commander Stagg has written about the different parts of Norway, their history, their landscape and their different characteristics. It is a sad thought that he did not live to see this last book printed. He was, as it has been said, one of the best friends Norway ever had in Great Britain.

The present volume deals with the Sørland, the country stretching from the old towns of Tønsberg to Stavanger. It is a country which has become the summer resort of the Norwegians, in warm summers an ideal country for bathing and sailing, which is now becoming popular also among foreign tourists. Commander Stagg knew its history, both political and social, from the earliest periods onwards and tells it simply and interestingly. The reader will, when he has finished this book, have a knowledge not only of the Sørland, but also of many of the notable events in Norway's long history. Norwegians too will read the book with profit and pleasure.

ALF SOMMERFELT

ACKNOWLEDGMENTS

I would like to express my heartfelt thanks and gratitude to Dr. Ada Polak and Mr. Carl Hambro, Cultural Councillor to the Royal Norwegian Embassy, who read through the typescript which my husband finished shortly before he died and who also assisted in the selection of the illustrations. I also wish to thank Professor Alf Sommerfelt and Mr. Gunne Hammarstrøm of the B.B.C. Norwegian Section, for kindly reading the proofs. Without their kind help in every way, this fifth and last book on the history of Norway would never have been published.

My grateful thanks are also due to the publishers for their kindness and courtesy to me.

MARJORIE STAGG

CONTENTS

PART V

ILLUSTRATIONS

Grateful acknowledgement is made for the use of the following photographs :

To K. TEIGEN FOT. for Plates 3b, 4a, 4b, 6a, 9a, 9b, 10b, 13a.

To MITTET FOTO A/S, for Plates 6b, 7, 12a, 12b, 13b, 15a.

To GYLDENDAL NORSK FORLAG for Plate 8a.

To WILSE, OSLO, for Plates 3a, 5b.

To O. VAERING, FOT. for Plate 11b.

To WIDERØE'S FLYVESELSKAP OG POLARFLY for plate 5a.

To ANDERS BAERHEIM, for Plate 14b.

To MRS. A. POLAK, for Plate 10a.

To WALDEMAR EIDE, for Plate 15b.

To UNIVERSITETETS OLDSAKSAMLING, for the frontispiece and Plate 2b.

PART I

VESTFOLD

CHAPTER I

THE PROVINCE OF VESTFOLD

The Kingdom of Vestfold

ALTHOUGH the Province of Vestfold is the smallest in all Norway, its traditions, legends and history are perhaps richer than those of any other fylke. Moreover, its capital city of *Tønsberg* is unquestionably the oldest town in the country—many thrilling events have occurred within its town limits, and fascinating historical ghosts still roam around its Castle Hill (Slottsfjellet) and wander about its streets.

Since *Jordanes* made no mention of 'vestfaldingi' when he named several tribes inhabiting Norway at the time he wrote his 'History of the Goths' (*ca.* A.D. 550), it would seem that Vestfold was not then an independent kingdom. It certainly became one during the course of the following two centuries, when its 'capital' would have lain at or near the site of the ancient mart of *Skiringsal*, where now stands the village of Tjølling. In the Viking Era and long before, Skiringsal was frequented by Frisian traders, who monopolized the sea-borne commerce of both Baltic and North Sea during several centuries.

Away in Sweden the royal family of *Ynglingene* at Uppsala were either eliminated or dispersed, and one of its scions, *Halvdan Hvitbein*, (whiteleg) founded a kingdom in East Norway (*ca.* 740). He and his son Eystein were both buried near the famous temple at Skiringsal in the middle of the eighth century. King Eystein married Hild, whose father, Erik Agnarson, was a Jute from Vendsyssel who had been ruling in Vestfold. There can be no doubt that Vestfold was subject to Jutish suzerainty for many years before and during Viking times (*ca.* 500–1016).

Eystein and Hild had a son *Halvdan the Gentle* who transferred (*ca.* 800) his 'capital' to Borre (Horten), where he lived on the farm of Holtan. It is possible that he made this move inland owing to the hostile attitude of the Vendsyssel kings, two of whom invaded Vestfold in 813. Halvdan the Gentle was so unfortunate—according to viking notions—as to die a natural death, when he was buried at Borre in what must surely have been one of the earliest barrows to be thrown up at that famous royal mausoleum.

His son *Gudrød Veidekonge*—the fourth 'yngling' king of Vestfold—having lost his first wife sent his High Steward to King Harald Rufus of Agder to demand the hand of the latter's daughter *Aasa.* He met with a blank refusal, and such an insult so incensed Gudrød that he put to sea with a large fleet, and arrived off Harald's 'palace' in Agder (Tromøy?) in the dead of night. He surprised and killed Harald and abducted Aasa—the girl who in due course became the mother of the renowned *Halvdan Svarte* (the black). When that baby was but a year old, Aasa contrived the murder of her husband and thus avenged her own father. Fears that her crime might bring reprisals on her head, caused her to flee to her old home in Agder; there she remained for some seventeen years, until her boy had grown to man's estate.

During the period of Halvdan Svarte's infancy and adolescence, his stepbrother *Olav Geirstadalv* ruled over Vestfold, until the moment came when—for some reason unknown—that kingdom was divided between them. According to Snorre, Olav retained the southern districts of the fylke, where he lived in his 'hall' at Geirstad: that place abuts on *Gokstad* (near Sandefjord), where the unique ship-burial was unearthed in 1880. The human remains found therein are believed to be the skeleton of Olav Geirstadalv who died *ca.* 840—they show he was a sufferer from osteoarthritis in knee and ankle, and consequently the dead man has our sympathy even after the lapse of eleven centuries.

When that magnificent funeral had taken place at Gokstad, Olav's son *Ragnvald* succeeded to his share of Vestfold. Nothing is known of King Ragnvald, except that *Ynglingatal* was composed in his honour—probably by Tjodolv of Kvina. No doubt he was a great prince in his generation. On Ragnvald's death *Halvdan Svarte* took over all Vestfold, and buried his mother,

Aasa, in the *Oseberg* ship, near Tønsberg (*ca.* 850) with such a wealth of treasure as to astound us in the twentieth century. Halvdan Svarte, before he was drowned in Randsfjord (*ca.* 865), recovered the dominions of his grandfather, and ruled over much of Østlandet. All these kingdoms were inherited by his son of immortal fame, *Harald Fairhair*.

The 'Ynglinge' kings of Vestfold come down to us through the sagas, but even more vividly by their monuments in Vestfold. At Borre, near Horten, lay the mausoleum of many kings—the most imposing collection of royal graves in all northern Europe: to the same group belong those other mighty barrows at Oseberg, Sem and Gokstad. The ship-graves of the ninth century provide clear evidence of great power and ambition: it is quite impossible that such richly furnished graves could have entombed mere local petty kings in Vestfold. They evidence a dignified origin for that royal family which created the united Kingdom of Norway. Other scions besides Harald Fairhair were Turgeis—the mighty viking chieftain who founded Dublin (*ca.* 850)—and Olav the White. They were members of the 'Ynglinge' family of Vestfold and natives of that province.

Danish Suzerainty in the Ninth Century

The saga hints at a weak rule in Vestfold in early ninth century, and confirmation of this appears in the Frankish Annals which state that two Jutish kings—Harald Klak and Reginfred, who were acclaimed in Jutland in 812—transported their forces to Vestfold (813) 'to the uttermost part of their dominions, because the chiefs and people there would not recognize them as their kings.' Vestfold was yet again subjected by them: kings in Denmark had obviously been exercising supremacy over the southern shores of Norway for several years previously.

The Danes were experiencing difficult times with the Franks at the close of the eighth and beginning of the ninth centuries, and their king Gotfred (Godefridus—a member of the 'Yngling' family) was murdered in Stifla Sound (probably on the coast of Vestfold) in 810, at which time he was recognized as supreme lord not merely over Denmark, but of all Viken and Värmland.

It seems clear that the expedition of 813 to Vestfold was undertaken to reassert a former sovereignty which threatened to break down at a critical moment.

It seems equally certain that the Danish hold on Viken had slipped before 840, and it is probable that by that date Halvdan Svarte had reunited Viken and the Opplands under his sceptre and—at all events temporarily—gained the advantage over his Danish masters. One of the rare occasions when the actual homeland of the Viking raiders is given in the Frankish Annals occurred in 843, when with a fleet of sixty-seven ships the *vestfaldingi* attacked Nantes on the Loire. This indicates a Norwegian kingdom in Vestfold possessed of considerable power—was it Halvdan Svarte's? Moreover, those 'vestfoldinger' proceeded to plunder Cadiz, as also Arzila in Morocco—so that booty they brought back to their Vestfold homes must have been fabulous. It can be no mere coincidence that Vestfold, together with part of Romerike, are the only areas in Østlandet which have disgorged large quantities of Irish bric-à-brac from the ninth century.

At times the Vestfold Kingdom embraced all Norway between the Glomma and Randsfjord, from Gudbrandsdal down to Gothenburg; the royal graves at Borre house the remains of its rulers. It was the rising power in Østlandet at the time that the Vestland kings were utilizing all their resources to seize land in Scotland and Ireland. Yet this Kingdom of Vestfold was never a stable one, since with each change of monarch risings are reported in the sagas of petty kings and leaders, who yet again had to be brought under the sceptre of Vestfold.

Very little is known about *Halvdan Svarte*, since his saga was so obviously written up from the most meagre data. After he met his death under the ice on Randsfjord (*ca.* 865) his body was quartered, and one section found its shrine somewhere within his Kingdom of Vestfold. His relations with his young son Harald Fairhair seem never to have been very cordial.

The Market at Skiringsal

The earliest market place in Vestfold was the small island of

Bjerkøy lying off Nøtterøy. It was one of the Frisian 'bezirk' which they established around the coasts of the North Sea and Baltic at the dawn of our Era—the most famous of them being 'Birka' (on the site of modern Stockholm) and Hedeby (Slesvig). At some remote date Bjerkøy mart was transferred to *Skiringsal*, and later still—in the ninth century—to Tønsberg. That town claims A.D. 871 as its foundation year.

Although Skiringsal ceased to be the place of residence of Vestfold's royal family after *ca.* 800, it continued nevertheless to function as the great Frisian mart: Ottar (Othere) from Haalogaland said that he had called there on his way to England where he told his tale to Alfred the Great (*ca.* 875), when he probably unloaded his cargo at 'Billings Gate'—the watergate in the Roman wall of London. A property at Viksfjord in Tjølling is still called 'Kaupang' (market), where markets would have been held on fixed dates during the summer—no doubt in conjunction with sacrifices at the temple where people from all over Viken would have attended. The name 'Saxavik' recalls that the Saxons frequented this mart.

No fewer than 115 barrows were still to be seen around Tjølling as recently as 1867—all thrown up during the ninth and tenth centuries—and thus it came about that a 'built-up area' grew around the market-place, which, however, faded away early in the eleventh century.

As for the commodities which were traded at those ancient marts, it is certain from 'finds' that Frankish jewellery and Flemish swords were imported in quantities—Tjodolv of Kvina in his saga referred to the sword as 'a fleming.' Various articles of foreign production and manufacture passed through the coastal marts to the 'kaupang' at Hamar, Nes, Storelvdalen and Trondheim. The Frisian vessels picked up return cargoes—largely of timber, furs and skins—at Tjølling and Portør. As it is known that Sem—now *Jarlsberg*—was a 'kongsgaard' as early as the time of Halvdan Svarte, it is probable that his mother, Aasa, bought her ornaments from Frisian and other foreign merchants at Tønsberg and Skiringsal. Many of them were buried with her in the *Oseberg* ship—that beautiful yacht-like craft must often have moored at the ancient quays at both those market-places.

The Reign of Harald Fairhair (865–933)

When Harald Fairhair succeeded his father (*ca.* 865) he was in his teens, but his maternal uncle made an excellent 'regent.' The two collected a strong force in Harald's paternal kingdoms, and marched it across the Dovrefjell on conquest bent. After seven years of bitter struggle Harald won the decisive Battle of Hafrsfjord (*ca.* 872—though some modern historians date it to about 890), and in the glory of that victory took a Danish princess, Ragnhild, to wife. He made Avaldsnes, near Haugesund, his headquarters and seldom visited Østlandet, though the saga states 'he came to Tønsberg where there is a market.' Harald transplanted the religious practices and way of life of his 'Ynglinge' forbears to Vestlandet, where no similar customs or beliefs had previously been observed.

The administration of Vestfold during Harald Fairhair's reign was carried on at the '*Haugating*'—the parliament of the fylke. It was held on the estate of Haugar, the old name of Møllebakken in the heart of modern Tønsberg—that town's name was spelt *Tunsberg* until the fifteenth century, and derives from the 'berg' of *Slottsfjellet* (the castle hill) which dominated Tønsberg.

Harald produced an astounding number of sons, for many of whom he tried to find employment as petty kings. To Bjørn he gave control of Vestfold, where he lived at the 'hall' at Sem and supervised the marts at Skiringsal and Tønsberg. He himself owned several ships trading overseas, which earned him the nickname of '*farmann*'—though he was often styled Bjørn Kaupmann (merchant).

When Harald Fairhair was ageing he appointed his son *Erik Blood-axe* to be suzerain over all his countless half-brothers, whom Harald had begotten from numerous 'lights-o'-love.' Even before the old king had gone to his rest, Erik Blood-axe started to eliminate such of his half-brothers as stood in the way of his obtaining sole control of all Norway, which he and his

Queen Gunhild—of evil reputation—were determined to acquire. One of the first to fall was Bjørn Farmann, who was surprised in the dead of night by King Erik and murdered with several of his followers (927). Snorre states that he lies in the barrow called 'Farmannshaugen,' some 400 yards south of the mansion of Sem (Jarlsberg), but excavation has yielded no human remains or ship.

After Harald's death (933) one son, *Olav Digerbein*, set himself up as overlord of all Viken, and another, Halvdan, of all Trøndelag. The two brothers met at Tønsberg to concoct plans to defy King Erik, but the latter caught them both unawares in the very act of plotting against him, and laid them low. Snorre, who says that Erik dealt the fatal blows with his own hand, appears to have heard the tradition when he was visiting Tønsberg in 1218 and describes the fight in detail, closing with a statement that they were buried on Møllebakken. It is possible that the barrow still called 'Farmannshaugen' is a cenotaph to commemorate the fact that 'Erik killed both his brothers in Tønsberg during the winter following Harald Fairhair's death (933).

Christianity is Brought to Vestfold

Two small 'blue-blooded' boys escaped the wrath of King Erik by fleeing to the Opplands. They were Tryggve, son of Olav Digerbein, and Gudrød, son of Bjørn Farmann: they remained in hiding until Erik Blood-axe fled to England. *Haakon (I) the Good* returned from the Court of Athelstan at Winchester and restored his two nephews to their rightful inheritances—*Gudrød* took over Vestfold, and ruled more or less independently throughout the reign of Haakon I (933–961).

Eight years after the latter king was killed at Fitjar, King Gudrød was murdered by *Harald Graafeld* near Tønsberg (969), the latter king having assumed paramountcy over the other 'sons of Gunhild'—the lady whom the chroniclers have painted in such deep black. In the following year King *Harald Bluetooth*, accompanied by old Haakon Ladejarl and *Harald Grenske* (a son of the murdered King Gudrød), came to Tønsberg with a large fleet. The Danish king was acclaimed 'King of Norway' at Haugating (970), and after that formal recognition of his rights to the country, he granted *Harald Grenske* the 'sub-kingship' of Vestfold, Agder and Vingulmark—he to pay tribute to Harald Bluetooth. Thus it had been established that all Viken—between Gothenburg and Lindesnes—was an integral part of Denmark, though it continued to be administered by petty kings until the arrival of Olav II (the Saint).

On the Jellinge stone near Vejle, Jutland, Harald's own words can be read in runes: 'I am that Harald who conquered all Denmark and Norway and christened the Danes.' He had been urged by the Emperor Otto II to spread Christianity, and two missionaries supported by an armed force arrived in a Vestfold whose traders had already come in contact with Christian communities overseas. That old heathen Haakon Ladejarl had, however, no sympathy with his ally's adherence to the Christian Faith, and 'passed through Viken ravaging as though it had been a foreign land.'

After the death of Harald Bluetooth, the *Jomsvikings* came to Norway at the behest of Svein Forkbeard of Denmark: they plundered Tønsberg on their way north to meet defeat at the hands of Haakon Ladejarl at *Hjørungavaag* (985).

When *Olav (I) Tryggvesson* recovered his father's (Tryggve Olavsson) Oppland kingdom (995) he found Viken already peopled by a Christian folk, and hence not needing the application of the harsh methods of conversion which, in his religious fervour, Olav enforced on other parts of his kingdom of Norway. A fantastic story is, however, told in the saga that Olav I shut up all the local 'medicine men' in these parts in a dwelling and set it alight. All were burnt to death except a certain Eyvind Kjelda, who succeeded in crawling to safety through the smoke-vent in the roof.

Olav Tryggvesson married the Danish Princess Tyra—probably at Tønsberg in 999—after his return from his abortive wooing of that frightful female Queen *Sigrid Storraade* of Sweden. Olav I perished at the Battle of Svolder (1000), whereupon King Svein Forkbeard of Denmark annexed Vestfold,

2. The Oseberg ship in the mound

Bronze Age cairn at Mölen

3. Jarlsberg Manor House, Sem

Sem Church

Grenland and Agder as far as Lindesnes. He then appointed Haakon Ladejarl's two sons, Erik and Svein, as his 'earls' over those territories, and it is on record that Earl Svein was judge in a case of murder at Tønsberg in 1015.

Saint Olav and Vestfold

King *Olav Haraldsson*—who was to become the saviour of Norway and its national saint—was a child of Ringerike, and so in this volume most of the legend, romance and history which cling to his name in South Norway is related in the story of *Buskerud* fylke (see p. 87).

Olav sailed from his mother's home in Ringerike with twenty-four ships to Tønsberg in the spring of 1016, accompanied by his step-father *Sigurd Syr* and other Oppland chiefs. They met and annihilated the fleet of Svein Ladejarl and Einar Tambarskjelver in the Battle of *Nesjar*—probably in Helgeroa Bay (Brunlanes)—on Palm Sunday, 25th March.

Olav's victory was overwhelming, and Svein fled to Sweden where he died within twelve months, whilst all the Danish 'sysselmenn' who had functioned in Viken almost continuously for half a century decamped to Denmark. Thereafter Olav II was acclaimed king throughout all Norway.

Snorre paints a striking picture of life in Tønsberg in the year 1018, in which he tells of the attempt by King Rørek to assassinate Olav. After the latter king had variously disposed of the five petty kings at Ringsaker in Hedmark,* and had caused the eyes of King Rørek to be gouged out, he brought that blind old warrior—'the wisest of all kings'—to Tønsberg where he took him to church on Ascension Day (1018). Sigvat Skald observed him in the act of stabbing Olav during divine service, but although the latter's dress was badly slashed he was not wounded. Olav's revenge was not death, as was to have been expected, but exile to Greenland, whither an Icelander named Torarin was deputed to convey him. Blind Rørek never reached his distant prison since he died in Iceland *en route*.

Olav II was in Tønsberg yet again in 1022, when he sum-

* See 'East Norway and its Frontier.'

moned the mighty Rogaland chief *Erling Skjalgsson* to attend; he arrived with a strong bodyguard. This compelled Olav to effect a compromise, but good relations were never established and open enmity soon broke out between them.

It was whilst Olav was in Tønsberg in 1025 that—according to Snorre—emissaries arrived from Canute the Great demanding his sovereign rights over the Kingdom of Norway. Olav's reply was: 'I will defend Norway with my sword as long as I live and will pay tribute to no man for my kingdom.' War soon broke out between the two kings, when Erling Skjalgsson manifested his hostility to Olav by sending his two sons to Canute in England—and by following them shortly afterwards. When Olav received intelligence that Canute was fitting out a large expeditionary force, he endeavoured to mobilize his own forces; few, however, responded except for his loyal Vestfold followers.

When Canute reached Trondheim he set up Haakon Eriksson Jarl as 'viceroy,' and then sailed south to a defenceless Tønsberg where he was acclaimed king at Haugating before continuing his voyage to Denmark in the autumn of 1028. As soon as Olav heard of Canute's departure from Tønsberg he sailed there with only thirteen ships but, as the remainder of his crews deserted, he had perforce to sail north with that slender strength and was destined never to see South Norway again.

South Norway was not directly concerned in the Battle of *Stiklestad*, except for the presence there of a few 'telemarkinger' whom Olav had managed to recruit. Before Olav the Saint died in that his last battle (1030), Svein—son of Canute—and his English mother Alfifa, together with other representatives of Canute, had reached Viken and passed on to Trondheim in the autumn of that year.

For the ensuing century Vestfold appears to have been in eclipse; at all events records are very meagre of events there. *Harald Haardraade* founded his own city of Oslo, which he made his base for campaigns against Denmark and to overawe the rebellious opplendinger. His two successors, Olav (III) Kyrre and Sigurd (I) Jorsalfar, seem to have clung to Eastern

Viken: indeed the latter founded his own town of *Konghelle* (near modern Gothenburg) and made of it a stronghold on the southern frontier of Norway.

Tønsberg was assuredly headquarters for the first bishops of Viken, who would have lived at *Teie* (Teigar) on Nøtterøy. Even after the See of Oslo was founded and a 'palace' built in that town, Teie continued to be the summer residence of the bishops of Oslo as late as the Reformation. Saxo Grammaticus makes it clear that in his time Tønsberg was an ecclesiastical centre.

Art in Vestfold's Early Days

The 'Vendel' style from Uppsala was paramount throughout Østlandet during the seventh century, with its elegant lines and massive decorative animal heads. This style swept westwards as far as England, and examples of its productions were found at Sutton Hoo in Suffolk when that seventh century ship-grave was excavated in 1939. *Borre* near Horten possessed a wealth of barrows from the 'Vendel' period, but the first outstanding excavation in Vestfold was that at *Gokstad*, near Sandefjord, in 1880. The ocean-going trading vessel there was 80 feet long and of oak—in perfect condition: it now lies in the Museum at Bygdøy, Oslo.

It was, however, from the *Oseberg* ship—excavated 1904 near Tønsberg—that the finest art treasures of the ninth century were unearthed, and it may well be that the 'kongsgaard' near Oseberg was the most important '*atelier*' for creations of the new artistic style of the Viking Age, which has with every justification been named '*Osebergstilen.*' It was a yacht-like vessel for use in enclosed waters—a royal barge. Two female skeletons lay within, one of whom was without doubt a servant who was sacrificed to attend on her mistress in the other world. Thirteen horses, six dogs and a young bullock, together with a bull's head, were also entombed to provide the dead lady with transport and necessities for hunting when she should have crossed the River Styx. A similar number of horses and dogs were buried in the *Gokstad* ship, which also contained a peacock. There has been no 'find' anywhere in Europe with such an inventory from the time of Charlemagne to compare with those in Vestfold, and these ship-graves give us a detailed picture of life and beliefs of the Viking Age people.

This vogue in art continued to be the ruling one until the middle of the tenth century, up till when it has been named '*Borrestilen*': it is remarkable for heavy ornamentation in both silver and bronze, but is also well represented in wood-carving—particularly in the Gokstad ship.

Modifications in style were introduced after Haakon (I) the Good brought ideas from England (*ca.* 940) to which the name '*Jellingestilen*' has been given, since the stone bearing that name near Vejle in Jutland—which was erected by Harald Bluetooth the Christian—is decorated with that type of motif.

When Christian teachings really began to affect artistic production the so-called '*Ringerikstilen*' was introduced—the name being derived from a group of decorated stone monuments especially prominent in Ringerike. The principal motifs are leaves on their stalks, woven together and looking amazingly natural. This style continued to be the vogue during the reign of St. Olav at beginning of eleventh century. Then new cultural influences began to assert themselves in Norway.

CHAPTER II

THE CIVIL WAR IN VESTFOLD

It was in 1126 that *Harald Gille* (Gilchrist—an Irishman or perhaps Hebridean) paid his first visit to *Sigurd* (*I*) *Jorsalfar* at the 'kongsgaard' of Sem, and claimed recognition as his brother. He had powerful friends in *Kale Kolsson* of Agder (see p. 135) and Hallkel Huk of Blindheim, whom he had met in Grimsby. Owing to the latter's representations to King Sigurd, it was agreed that Harald should undergo the trial of 'ordeal by fire' to establish his claim that he was a natural son of Magnus II (Barefoot). The King took the precaution to extract a solemn oath from Harald before undergoing the ordeal, that he would not advance his claim to the throne until both Sigurd himself and his son Magnus III (the Blind) were dead.

It was in the very church at Sem which stands today that Harald Gille walked barefoot across nine heated ploughshares—calling all the while to St. Columba for strength and support. After crossing the ninth and last ploughshare he threw himself on a couch which had been prepared. There his feet were bandaged, and when three days later the wrappings were removed the soles of his feet were undamaged. After such a witness from the Almighty, King Sigurd accepted Harald Gille as a brother, and that fraternal adoption lit the spark which touched off the *Great Civil War* which raged for more than a century and bled Norway almost to death.

Whilst Sigurd was at Tønsberg in the summer of 1129, he granted half the Orkneys to Kale Kolsson, and appointed him his 'earl' under the name of *Ragnvald* (see p. 135). On Sigurd's death (1130) Harald took counsel with Kale and with his father Kol, who advised him to summon 'Haugating' and break his oath to Sigurd that he would not claim the throne whilst Magnus (III) was alive. *Harald Gille* was duly acclaimed, and assembled such a powerful 'hird' that Magnus came to terms and surrendered one-half of the kingdom. It was, however, an uneasy partnership, and after Harald's defeat at Fyrileiv (1134) he fled to Denmark, whose king provided reinforcements with which he eventually returned to Tønsberg—to receive a great welcome. Magnus had foolishly withdrawn his forces to Bergen and thus left the field in Viken clear for Harald.

When Harald was murdered at Bergen by *Sigurd Slembe*, the latter met violent opposition in Vestfold, where Harald's two infant sons were recognized. Their grand champion at that time was Vatn-Orm, who is remembered owing to his unfortunate encounter with Sigurd Slembe in the harbour of Portør. Then his mantle fell upon his brother, *Gregorius Dagsson*, who faithfully upheld the cause of King Inge I through a quarter of a century until his death (1160). In the year that followed, that king was killed on the ice off Oslo by the forces of *Haakon II* (Herdebreid), who sailed to Tønsberg where he was attacked by *Erling Skakke* and lost all his craft—including 'Bøkesuden' which had been King Inge's flagship.

After that decisive victory at Tønsberg all Viken and Vestlandet adhered to Erling Skakke, who returned from his victory over King Haakon at Sekken in Romsdalfjord still more triumphant in 1162. He was quite prepared to encounter the dead Haakon's faithful followers when they arrived at Ramnes (Re)—some ten miles north-west of Tønsberg—under the command of 'riksjarlen' *Sigurd of Røyr*. Erling did not defy the dictates of chivalrous custom by attacking during the hours of darkness, but surprised his enemy at daylight, when by employing a ruse he tempted Sigurd away from his strong position. Sigurd fell in this first Battle of Re (1163) together with sixty of his men, and Erling Skakke repaired to Tønsberg where he stayed the rest of the year.

Valdemar the Great of Denmark had planned a campaign in Viken to assert his claim to the sovereignty of Viken as far west as Rygjarbit. He was acclaimed at Borgarting (Sarpsborg) during the summer of 1165, and then proceeded to Tønsberg where he met strong opposition. It had been Valdemar's intention to burn the town, but he refrained in order not to desecrate its churches. He then summoned Haugating but no representatives attended and even the local priests patriotically abstained. After a parley with *Orm Kongsbror*, Valdemar departed without taking hostile action.

Two years later Erling Skakke began hostilities with Denmark, which caused Valdemar to renew his attacks on Viken (1168) in support of Olav Ugjeva (the unlucky)—an enemy of Erling's. Saxo Grammiticus and Archbishop Absalon of Copenhagen accompanied Valdemar on this expedition, and after Erling had abandoned 'Slottsfjellet' Valdemar climbed to its plateau to admire its defensive potentialities. Erling had, however, taken up a strong position at *Vrengen*, which he blocked with a boom, so when Valdemar held a conference a majority of his advisers resolved that as Denmark was such a fat land compared to Norway the latter country might be left alone. Then, despite the protests of the Archbishop, Valdemar sailed away to Portør and along Agdesiden, until dissatisfaction among his crews induced him to return to their homeland. He then instituted a blockade of the coast of Viken, which caused such a shortage of corn in Norway that Erling proceeded to Denmark to negotiate. Peace was concluded (1170) after Erling had sworn fealty for his 'earldom' of Viken—a formal subservience to the Crown of Denmark which was entirely meaningless.

Nine years passed by without any record of events, until *Eystein Møyla* arrived at Ramnes with the first members of that famous insurgent band which later was to gain such a reputation under the name of '*birchlegs*.' Just as had happened in 1163, a force led by *Magnus IV* and Orm Kongsbror marched from Tønsberg to Ramnes, and attacked the 'birchlegs.' Eystein sought refuge in the home of a peasant whom he begged to spare his life, but the latter killed him and carried the corpse to King Magnus (1177). Ramnesgaard was used as royal headquarters at both battles of *Re*.

Sverre paid his first visit to Vestfold in 1176, to find out whether he might expect to receive support there. He learnt that 'all the people were true and faithful to King Magnus'—who often resided at Tønsberg. When, two years later, Sverre took his ships to Drammenselva, Magnus led a force to break up his 'birchlegs,' but was himself taken by surprise in Lier and suffered heavy losses. Throughout the period of dispute with Sverre, Tønsberg was ever a stronghold of Magnus, who returned there after his last period of exile in Denmark (1184) with twenty-six vessels. A month later Magnus was killed and utterly defeated at *Fimreite* in Sogn.*

Sverre then temporarily subdued all Viken which, however, broke into revolt against him in the year following under the leadership of *Jon Kuvlung*, a reputed son of Inge I, who was acclaimed at 'Haugating' (1185). After Jon had experienced considerable successes at Bergen and Trondheim, he was defeated off Jaeren (1187) and fled to Tønsberg. Sverre arrived there in the autumn of 1188 and seized all the 'kuvlunger' ships. Then Jon and his kuvlunger marched overland to Trondheim, captured its castle, seized Sverre's ships there, and sailed to Bergen. Sverre appeared on the scene just before Xmas and killed Jon Kuvlung, whereupon his followers dispersed; thus ended the first attempt to found a 'Kingdom of East Norway.'

Sverre's brother, Erik, was at that time his 'earl' in Viken, and had to face a new enemy (vaarbelger) who were aided by Denmark. Sixteen of their ships were indulging in a plunder raid, when the seamen of Tønsberg utterly defeated them among the Hvaløyer. Erik, his wife and son all died of poisoning when living at St. Olav's Abbey, Tønsberg, whereupon Sverre himself took over direct control of Vestfold.

It was in 1191 that a body of Danish and Norwegian crusaders, with the 'birchleg' chief Ulv of Lauvnes in company, came to Tønsberg to careen their ships. One of the party wrote a vivid description of the town and its inhabitants and they sailed away with the blessings of everybody. For reasons unknown Sverre wanted to negative this crusade and instructed Ulv of Lauvnes to lead them up the garden path.

Two years later a second band of rebels called 'Island-beards' (Øyskjeggene) arrived unexpectedly at Tønsberg and killed Sverre's nephew Jon. They summoned Haugating, where Sigurd (son of Magnus IV) was acclaimed king—probably by repre-

* See 'West Norway and its Fjords.'

sentatives from all Viken. That band of rebels remained at Tønsberg until the following summer, when they sailed to Bergen where they were annihilated—and Sigurd killed—at the Battle of *Florevaag* (1194).

* * * * *

A new phase in the Great Civil War opened when the first '*bagler*' were recruited by *Bishop Nicholas Arnesson*—with Sigurd Jarlson (a son of Erling Skakke) and Reidar Sendemann as their generals. Not until 1197 did Sigurd arrive at Tønsberg where he killed Sverre's brother; all Viken was in arms against Sverre who was never *persona grata* in that area, and Bishop Nicholas preached vehemently against him.

When Sverre fought his great battle at Oslo, the men of Tønsberg sailed there fully expecting to be met by a triumphant peasantry, but were instead received by a victorious Sverre, and most of the 'vestfoldinger' were slaughtered as they slipped about helplessly on the ice, since, unlike Sverre's men, they had not 'studded' their footwear.

After that reverse, the 'bagler' made Tønsberg their capital, and 'Slottsfjellet' their citadel—with *Reidar Sendemann* in command of that stronghold. In 1201 Sverre brought a strong force from Bergen and invested Slottsfjellet, where Reidar Sendemann had a garrison of 200 men. Having failed to take the hill by storm, Sverre opened a regular siege and his auxiliaries (guests) under *Peter Steyper* transported complete houses from the town and re-erected them to the north of Slottsfjellet—that spot continued to be known for centuries as 'Gjestebakken' (the guests hill). Thus was Slottsfjellet cut off from the outside world.

It was whilst the siege was in progress that the notorious *ribbalder* arrived at Tønsberg—a body of 150 barbarian Welsh archers whom Sverre had recruited through the good offices of King John of England. Having landed in Bergen those cut-throats crossed the mountains into Hallingdal, and then via Sokndal, Telemark, and Grenland into south-west Vestfold. Wherever they passed they committed every conceivable bestiality—'killed young and old, women as well as men, destroyed all living creatures that crossed their path and burnt every dwelling in sight. When, however, any strong body of peasants stood up to them, they fled to the mountains, and turned up where least expected . . . nobody had ever seen such Devil's work committed.' They fought bravely for Sverre and were excellent archers—but the memory of the Welsh 'ribbalder' was cursed in South Norway for many years to come.

At long last hunger on Slottsfjellet became so acute that a captain was sent down to Sverre to ask for 'safe conduct.' As this was conceded Reidar surrendered after an epic resistance of twenty weeks—at the end of January 1202. He swore fealty to Sverre and lay sick for a long while, during which illness Sverre did all that was possible to save his life—and Reidar lived to fight another day. Not so Sverre, for he picked up some infection during his stay in Tønsberg and died in Bergen as a result.

Reidar Sendemann was a picturesque figure, who had returned from service with the 'varangs' at Constantinople in 1195, bringing a letter from its Emperor Alexis imploring Sverre to provide him with military assistance to use against his brother. When Sverre gave Reidar permission to recruit, the latter ran across Bishop Nicholas Arnesson who was then raising forces in Skaane for his 'bagler' army. After Sverre had gone to his rest (1202), Reidar and his brother-in-law Peter Steyper—both of whom had married daughters of King Magnus IV—played vital roles during the confused period that ended with the *Truce of Kvitesøy* (1208). They had no relish for a life in a Norway at peace, so both went to Jerusalem with their wives. Reidar later took service with the Emperor of Byzantium, and died at Constantinople in 1214; thus perished the hero of the greatest of all Tønsberg's military exploits.

The Kingdom of East Norway

Tønsberg became the royal capital of the '*Kingdom of East Norway*,' and thither came young *Erling Steinvegg*—a son of Magnus IV—to be subjected to 'ordeal by fire.' Bishop Nicholas Arnesson was particularly desirous that this trial should be undergone in the presence of Valdemar II (Sejr), who arrived at Tønsberg with 300 vessels on 17th June, 1204. It was Valdemar who decided the manner of the ordeal and administered the oath, whilst the bishop determined its heat content and applied the hot iron. Valdemar caused the church to be surrounded by armed men during the crucial moments of removal of the bandages, whilst King and Bishop remained within the church. The latter remarked that he 'had never seen a hand come away so unscathed' —and then all sang *Te Deum Laudamus*.

Erling was acclaimed at Haugating on the following day, and both King Erling and Earl Philip (nephew of Bishop Nicholas) paid fealty to Valdemar as suzerain over the little kingdom, and gave hostages for their good behaviour. King Valdemar returned to Denmark shortly after just as peacefully as he had arrived. The 'bagler' were now lords in Viken, with Tønsberg for their royal capital and seat of their own king.

In the spring of 1205, however, the 'bagler' had to flee from Tønsberg when Haakon Galen approached with a strong force and succeeded in having *Inge II* acclaimed at Haugating. Whilst this was happening at Tønsberg, the 'bagler' had seized Trondheim, where both Erling and Philip were acclaimed at Øreting—an event which caused Haakon Galen to move north rapidly.

King Erling Steinvegg spent Christmas 1206–07 at Tønsberg, but died there the following February, leaving two sons who were but infants. So Duke Philip succeeded to the throne of East Norway. Fortunes swayed to and fro that year, and while the 'birchlegs' captured Tønsberg, King Philip received the surrender of Bergenhus, where he behaved with great gallantry to the noble 'birchleg ladies' whom he captured.

Then Bishop Nicholas arranged the Round Table meeting at *Kvitesøy* (1208), which gave Sverre's daughter *Kristin* as a bride to Philip, to thus cement the two factions in Norwegian public life. When she married Philip at Oslo in 1209 Kristin brought her husband as a dowry the Opplands and also Viken between Svinesund and Rygjarbit. When her mother—Sverre's Swedish widow—died a few days later, Philip came into vast properties in Värmland and Västergötland, whither he hurried to collect the loose cash.

Queen Kristin died in childbirth (1213) and the baby soon after, but having outlived its mother Philip inherited all her estates. Kristin had fought hard to procure a royal title for her husband, and as Sverre's daughter her word carried great weight with the 'birchlegs,' but after she had died childless there was no heir of Philip's to continue the line. Philip himself was an attractive personality and most popular: it was during his reign that the vassal relationship towards Denmark faded away.

When Inge II died, Philip sent a message to Duke Skule suggesting the division of the country between them—otherwise he would begin fighting all over again. However, while the messengers were actually speeding Philip became ill at Tønsberg, and died at Løvøy, near Horten, in July 1217. As soon as Haakon IV and Duke Skule learnt of Philip's death they hastened to Tønsberg to meet Bishop Nicholas, where a large gathering of representatives met in Maria church. They resolved on a truce between 'bagler' and 'birchlegs,' and determined that the former should retain half of the 'sysler' over which Philip had ruled.

Thus was the '*Kingdom of East Norway*' dissolved, and *Haakon IV* was acclaimed at Haugating: the long period of disunity and strife was brought to a halt, though much blood was yet to flow before the final settlement and the end of the last 'pretender.' Vestfold syssel came under 'bagler' rule—Oslo under 'birchleg': the former still considered Tønsberg to be their capital and its leaders dwelt there, including Arnbjørn Jonsson.

Soon afterwards the new 'rebel' pack called '*ribbunger*' gained the ascendancy in Viken whilst Haakon and Skule were in Trondheim, and Arnbjørn Jonsson had to hold 'Slottsfjellet' against them through the winter of 1221–22. Haakon arrived unexpectedly at Vrengen with a large fleet, and almost simultaneously Skule came from Oslo—likewise without warning. The 'ribbunger' were routed, but continued to make trouble for several years. Haakon had to campaign in Värmland to root out their lair, and on return to Tønsberg from that punitive expedition he received the first definite warning from Skule of a breach in their relations. Haakon thereupon hastened to Bergen to marry Skule's daughter Margaret in the hope that that union would satisfy the ambitious Duke—he was but twenty-one and his bride only seventeen. Together with the king's mother, Inga of Varteig, they returned to Tønsberg in the autumn (1225) and took up residence on Slottsfjellet.

After Sigurd Ribbung died (1226) his rebellion fizzled out and the defences of Tønsberg became of less importance, so the town was neglected to some extent by the national leaders, whilst Haakon kept Court at Bergen and Skule in Trondheim. Relations between them grew gradually worse, and had become tense when the King and Queen—together with her mother Ragnhild (wife of Skule)—arrived at Tønsberg in the spring of 1238 when Queen Margaret was expecting. On 3rd May the future Magnus V was born at Tønsberg.

The later engagements between Haakon and Skule did not affect Vestfold, except that after the defeat of the king's forces at Laake (Nannestad) his commanders took refuge at Tønsberg, where Arnbjørn Jonsson died after having given faithful service to his king through twenty years. Then came the moment when Haakon IV sailed through Vrengen on his way to Oslo to administer a final defeat upon Skule, which presaged his death at Trondheim (1240). The woeful century-long Great Civil War had at long last come to an end.

CHAPTER III

VESTFOLD IN LATE MIDDLE AGES

The Aftermath of the Civil War

AFTER Skule's death there followed a long spell of internal peace and national prosperity, during which Tønsberg continued to play an important role—both militarily and politically. Haakon IV and Magnus V erected fortifications on Slottsfjellet which made it the strongest position in all Norway for several years. Not until Haakon V built Akershus (*ca.* 1300) could Oslo compare with Tønsberg in military importance.

Relations between Haakon IV and Denmark grew strained, and whilst the latter country was split by internal dissensions a fleet assembled at Tønsberg (1253) to launch a campaign against her. The King of Denmark gave way on that occasion, but three years later no fewer than 360 vessels were collected at Tønsberg which proceeded to ravage the Province of Halland.

It was while he was returning north after that campaign that King Haakon met a Spanish Embassy, led by a priest named Ferdinand (see p. 137) who had been sent from Castile to solicit the hand of Haakon's daughter. The King invited them to proceed to Tønsberg, where he would send his reply before the spring. Hence it came about that the town gave hospitality to the Spaniards through the winter, and the young Crown Prince Haakon spent Christmas with them. That hopeful prince returned from yet another campaign against the Danes in Halland, to die at St. Olav's abbey in Tønsberg. The Spanish Embassy doctor attended but to no avail: his father took the body to St. Hallvard's, Oslo, where he was buried beside Sigurd Jorsalfar.

On the advice of his Council King Haakon agreed that his daughter *Kristina* should proceed to Spain, where she herself might select which of the Spanish princes she would marry. So the grand fleet set sail from Tønsberg, and Kristina chose the youngest son—Don Philip: the wedding was celebrated magnificently on 31st March, 1258. Her married life was short and unhappy: she died in 1262 aged but twenty-eight, probably at Covarrubias on the Castilian plateau, where a tomb is believed to be hers.

Haakon's disputes with Denmark came to an end when the Danish Princess Ingeborg crossed the Skagerak to marry Magnus V (1261). She was a fabulously wealthy heiress, but her Danish properties were to be the cause of many difficulties at a later date. King Haakon visited Tønsberg for the last time in the spring of 1262—he had originated the erection of many works in the town and on Slottsfjellet, and had dredged Skjelljastenssund (Stensund—now Kanalen) to admit the passage of craft by a more direct route to Oslo.

He and his son Magnus, however, made Bergen pre-eminently their capital city and it was there that Magnus V assembled all the notables in Norway (1273) in order to determine the spheres of authority of lendmenn and sysselmenn and their responsibility to the king. Then in 1277 came the celebrated '*Tønsberg settergerd*' (composition) to determine relations between Church and State. At a meeting in the Franciscan Abbey (King Magnus was ever an ardent supporter of that Order) a compromise was arrived at, the terms of which evidenced how strong the Church had become despite the victory which Sverre had gained over it. The decisions taken by that National Assembly—which became the universal law of Norway until the Reformation—are dated as from *Castrum Tunsbergense:* the MS. is in a splendid condition despite its existence through seven centuries. One provision of his 'universal' law was the affirmation of validity of *Tønsberg vekt* (Tønsberg weight)—a measure which the Frisians had brought to that town when it was the sole overseas mart in south Norway. It was based on the ancient 'Troy weight'—so named after that town in Champagne in the days of Charlemagne.

Troubles with Sweden were brewing during the reign of Magnus, so he built the famous tower called *Teglkastellet* (*ca.* 1275) on Slottsfjellet. He led a fleet to Sweden to try to compose dynastic disputes there, and on returning found many distinguished visitors at Tønsberg from the Orkneys, Shetlands and elsewhere overseas. Magnus V died in 1280.

When war broke out with the German cities in 1284, *Alv Erlingsson* (The Count of Sarpsborg) began a campaign of piracy. Although apparently a 'private' war there is little doubt that the Regency Council were behind 'Mindre Alv,' and the Germans retaliated with a blockade. This compelled King Erik II to sue for peace, but Tønsberg continued to play a role in Alv's piracies, and it was to that town his mangled remains were brought for burial after he had been broken on the wheel in Helsingborg (1290). 'Mindre Alv' had, however, no direct connexion with Vestfold (see p. 90) except for a doubtful tradition that he owned *Herre-Skjelbrei* in Høyjord, where he was wont to play fast and loose with the local ladies. The church spire at Høyjord is topped by a gilded weathervane which *legend* relates at one time defiantly challenged all-comers on the prow of 'Mindre Alv's' flagship.

When *Haakon V* made Oslo his capital city (1299), and Akershus Norway's premier fortress, it spelt the end of Tønsberg's leading position 'sønnenfjells.' Yet that great king issued thence his famous decree (1308) subordinating all thanes to royal authority, and appears to have spent his last winter at Tønsberg. The resultant effect of his celebrated decree against the nobility was such that there remained but a feeble upper-class to uphold the dignity of the Norwegian nation. He died at Tønsberg, after much suffering, on 8th May, 1319, when his body was borne to Oslo and buried in the Royal Chapel of Maria there.

Tønsberg in the Thirteenth Century

Slottsfjellet was fortified during the 1160's and was at that time thought to be invincible, though no curtain wall ringed it round until *ca.* 1230. Haakon IV built gatehouses and also a dwelling called *Bredestuen*, a royal 'hall' built of brick which lay close to *St. Michael's* Church but sufficiently removed from it as not to set the sacred building alight from kitchen sparks. St. Michael's was made a Chapel Royal by Haakon V: it was a frequented place of pilgrimage where dispensations could be purchased well into the fifteenth century. Queen Margaret the Great donated large sums for pilgrims in 1405, when one of her secretaries made a special journey there on her behalf.

The fortifications on Slottsfjellet were completed before the Black Death (1349). Decay set in during the fifteenth century, when both Knut Alvsson and Henrik Krummedike captured it without difficulty. A Swedish invasion (1503) coincided with an internal revolt, and led to its destruction—never to rise again.

Owing to its wealth of churches and ecclesiastical institutions Tønsberg was ever regarded as a 'holy' town and the Church kept alive a spiritual atmosphere. The principal church was *St. Laurence* (*ca.* 1120), which stood on the site of the present cathedral.

St. Olav's Premonstratensian abbey—which was mentioned by Danish crusaders in 1191—was a wealthy foundation. Its church was the largest *round church* in all the north, having 12 feet more diameter than the famous round church in Slesvig. Among the graves within it was that of King Erling Steinvegg (1207)—nothing now remains of the building except remnants of foundations, whose preservation the excellent City Council are ensuring. A 'hospital' was founded (*ca.* 1300) to administer to the needs of the numerous pilgrims: it continued to function until the great town fire of 1536.

There were two 'guilds' in Tønsberg—St. Anne and St. Olav—throughout the Middle Ages, at whose feasts men, women and children were present. Ale played a major role in the proceedings of St. Olav Guild: beakers were blessed to the honour of God the Father, Jesus Christ, the Holy Spirit and the Virgin Mary. One of its rules was: 'The feast shall continue so long as the brethren wish and the ale lasts'; the memory of those members who had passed on was solemnly 'skaaled.' A survival from heathen times, its purpose was to create a community spirit and to give social security to its members. The religious backing it received necessitated a procession to St. Olav's altar in St. Laurence Church.

The townsfolk earned their livelihood exporting timber, skins, hides and butter; trade with Novgorod had been carried on from Viking times. Rostock is first mentioned in 1260, but the upswing in German trade did not begin until the 1290's: throughout the fourteenth and fifteenth centuries the merchants of Rostock and Wismar shut out all other foreigners and suppressed the local trade of the towns. Trade with England was dwindling before 1300, in which year an agreement between a citizen of Tønsberg and a merchant of Holkham in Norfolk is recorded: this led to a dispute, when Edward I instructed his bailiffs to enquire into the matter. What really upset Anglo-Norwegian trade was the dastardly action of some English sailors (1312) who murdered a royal sheriff—probably at Lahelle on Nøtterøy—and the murdered man may well have been Tønsberg's commandant. This crime led to a complete cessation of trade with England for several years.

Tønsberg's very own Queen

When but a three-years-old infant little *Magnus VI* was acclaimed King of Sweden at 'Morating' and of Norway at 'Haugating'—with that formal act the 'ting' of Vestfold supplanted Tronheim's 'Øreting' as site of proclamation of Norway's monarch. Ingeborg, the mother of Magnus, continued to reside at Bredestuen on Slottsfjellet with her babe, until after the lapse of twelve months the Swedes demanded the presence of their king in their country.

The story of Ingeborg's scandalous behaviour does not concern South Norway: after she had dissipated most of the reserves accumulated by her father, Haakon V, quasi-regal powers were given to *Erling Vidkunnsson* as 'drottsete' in 1325 in the hope that he might save something from the wreck. After Ingeborg had married Knut Porse (1327) Tønsberg saw her no more since they retired to Denmark, but the town became the centre of the famous revolt led by Erling Vidkunnsson and the Haftorsonns in 1333 when they resisted King Magnus' proposals to go to war to reconquer Skaane. It was also at Tønsberg that the King yielded to the distinguished rebel leaders.

In 1334, when eighteen years of age, Magnus VI travelled to Namur with a number of Swedish courtiers in company, to seek the hand of *Blanche* (Blanca), daughter of Count John of Namur. Through her mother she was related to the royal family of France, and Edward III of England issued a safe conduct for the squadron which brought her to Norway in the autumn of 1335.

Tunsberghus was chosen for the wedding festivities owing to its buildings and equipment being more 'European' than those of the royal apartments at Oslo—though the table service had to be loaned from the nunnery at the latter city. Queen Blanche received as her wedding portion the fiefs of Tønsberg and Lødøse (Gothenburg). During the early years of marriage she had as 'Mistress of the Robes' that crazy Swedish woman who was later canonized as *Saint Birgitte* (Bridget): she is believed to have exercised a powerful influence on the young queen. Blanche had, however, brought with her a considerable measure of refreshing Continental culture to backward Norway—architecture and furnishings reveal a new influence. Floor-tiles bearing the *fleur-de-lys* have been unearthed, and that emblem was embodied in some escutcheons of the nobility of the two countries.

Yet another revolt broke out in 1388 when Magnus was scheming to arrogate to himself absolute power. Erling Vidkunnsson and other rebel leaders met at Tønsberg, where the Church hierarchy succeeded in mediating a peaceful solution.

Queen Blanche gave birth to a second son Haakon (later VI) in 1340: he spent his childhood in Tønsberg as his father had done, and there he lived through the *Black Death* (1349) which devastated Vestfold in like manner to the rest of Norway. The union of the two Crowns having become exceedingly unpopular it was agreed that young Haakon become the titular king of Norway, and in 1350 Magnus handed the young boy over to the care of the 'drottsete,' *Orm Eysteinsson*, and left for Sweden, which country he and his elder son Erik were to rule.

A rising of the Swedish aristocracy caused a complete breach between the royal couple and 'Saint' Birgitte who was a member of the 'upper ten.' That venomous female proceeded to foul the reputations of Magnus and Blanche with her poisonous scandal, and accused the former of homosexual practices which earned for him the scurrilous nickname '*Smeik*.' Blanche was accused of intimate relations with a Swedish noble, and even of having poisoned her own son Erik when he happened to die suddenly in 1359. The fact seems to be that they were a devoted couple, and it is known that Blanche was of a happy disposition with a lucid brain and great charm, who made an excellent consort for Magnus.

In 1353 Queen Blanche's wedding fiefs were exchanged for those of Østfold and Ranrike; thus with her fiefs in Värmland and Dalsland she held a continuous 'kingdom' between Oslofjord and Vänern, a mid-Scandinavian kingdom which at certain periods embraced all Borgartingslov—from Agder to Västergötland. Disunity in the Peninsula led to a series of intrigues, in which it would seem that the 'drottsete' got himself involved. So Orm Eysteinsson had to pay for his disloyalty—if that were his crime—with his head, which fell at Tønsberg. That town had become a political centre, and held that distinction for a quarter of a century until Magnus met his death by drowning in 1374.

The royal couple lived in Bredestuen and Teglkastellet when at Tønsberg, where Queen Blanche resided continuously after the death of her elder son in 1359. Then she travelled to Copenhagen to attend King Haakon VI's wedding with his child-queen Margaret (1363)—later to be known as 'Queen of the North.' When Blanche was taken ill on the return journey it was rumoured she had been poisoned at the wedding—she died that autumn at Tønsberg. Judging from the inventory of her chattels at death her way of life must have been terribly austere: one item reads 'two sheets which have often been on the bed'; another, 'two tablecloths which have often been on the table.' Surely such threadbare articles would have constituted only a portion of her household linen?—although the royal family is known to have been poverty-stricken.

A moving tribute to the memory of the gentle Queen Blanche has this year (1956) come from Namur, in the form of a letter from its Mayor to his equivalent at Tønsberg suggesting that the two cities adopt each other—to revive the memory of Blanche and reunite the link she forged more than six centuries ago.

The Last Years of Magnus VI

The rebels in eastern Sweden deposed Magnus and chose Albrecht of Mecklenburg as their king, whilst Magnus retained the western portion of that country. Two years after the death of his queen, Magnus was taken prisoner at the Battle of Gata (1365)—yet strange to relate he is known to have been in Tønsberg shortly afterwards. It is possible the Swedes released him *en parole* to enable him to put his affairs in order, and that he then returned to detention—no doubt he took oaths as well as leaving hostages behind. Henceforth Haakon VI rules his father's dominions in his own name.

The Hansa were extremely truculent for a whole decade, and Haakon had to face up to many difficulties. He succeeded in raising a revolt against Albrecht of Mecklenburg in eastern Sweden (1369), and later Magnus abandoned his pretentions to rule that part of the country. This secured the release of Magnus from captivity, and both kings were in Tønsberg (1372) to meet an embassy from the Hansa in St. Laurence Church. After protracted negotiations the Wendish cities of the Hansa obtained the restoration of their ancient trading privileges, they for their part giving assurances not to assist Albrecht of Mecklenburg. It was not until 1376—two years after the death of Magnus, that a final agreement was reached.

King Magnus VI was drowned near Haugesund (1374) at the age of fifty-nine. He must have been blessed with a robust constitution, since he seems to have been entirely unaffected by five years' rigorous imprisonment, or any the worse for constant travelling over his wide-flung dominions at a period when movement was not easy. The masses in Sweden clung to Magnus and styled him 'the honourable and good lord,' whilst he was well liked by the aristocracy of Norway and of those frontier districts in Sweden over which he ruled. As with so many celebrated characters who suffered misfortunes not of their own making, he was looked upon as 'holy' after his death: he was without any doubt an upright and well-meaning king, but lacked the gift of ruling which was so essential in his troubled era.

His memory is closely linked with Tønsberg since he spent much of his life there: in all probability he was buried in Maria Church, Oslo, by the side of his Queen Blanche. He retained the loyalty and affection of his son, Haakon VI through all his adversities.

The Fifteenth Century in Vestfold

Haakon VI took over his father's western Swedish provinces, which thus became temporarily united with Norway—with Tønsberg as their centre of administration. When Henry Sinclair, Earl of Orkney, visited Norway to receive his grant as 'earl' of those islands from Haakon VI, and to pay homage, he left behind at Tønsberg four Scots as hostages for his good behaviour, viz: William Dalziel, Malis Sparre, David Creighton and Alexander Rod.

King Haakon was buried in Maria church, Oslo (1380), and with his passing Tønsberg ceased to be a 'capital' in any sense of the word. Henceforward it was merely the chief town of Vestfold province—its national history was over and done with.

Queen *Margaret the Great* paid no heed to Vestfold throughout her regency, but *Erik of Pommern* was in Tønsberg (1405), whence he dispatched an embassy to England to seek the hand of Princess Philippa, the sister of Henry V of Agincourt.

During Østlandet's revolt against Erik (1436) its peasantry joined Amund Sigurdsson Bolt in his demand that Norway be governed solely by native-born Norwegians. An agreement was concluded on Jersøy whereby all foreign bailliffs should leave Norway before 29th July that same year.

In the confusion that followed the death of *Christoffer of Bayern* (1448), Tønsberg once again became a political storm centre. The commandant of Tønsberghus, *Erik Saemundsson*, led the party which desired to hand the Crown of Norway to

Karl VIII Knutsson of Sweden. When Karl was acclaimed at Hamar, he appointed Erik Saemundsson 'riksforstander' in South Norway. The other leaders of the Swedish party, however, deserted the cause of Karl and supported that of Christian I of Denmark. Hence it came about that the pro-Danish party won the day—and Erik Saemundsson paid for his loyalties with his life. His inveterate enemy was the Danish commandant at Akershus, *Hartvig Krummedike*, who acquired much wealth and influence through marrying the heiress of *Brunla* len, Skieno syssel and the whole of Agder: he owned no fewer than 27-farms in 1456.

Tønsberg lost any pretensions to be a royal town under the kings of the Danish Union—Christian I visited that town but once (1460). After his death (1480) Archbishop Gaute and the leading Norwegian counsellors met on Jersøy to determine Christian's successor, and a long period elapsed before they overcame their hesitation to elect King Hans—at Kalmar in 1483. He appointed Jon Smør 'drottsete,' but he was shortly afterwards drowned with his friend Einar Fluga off Jersøy—the latter reached shore alive, but died lying on a stone which legend states was 'red as blood.'

All Østlandet supported *Knut Alvsson's* rebellion * (1502) with the renewed demand that foreign bailiffs be evicted from Norway. Tønsberg and Akershus fell to Knut, and when *Henrik Krummedike* tried to recapture the former with Scottish mercenaries he was repulsed. The treacherous assassination of Knut Alvsson brought triumph to Krummedike and his Danes: Tønsberghus opened its gates to King Hans who reappointed Mattis Alsen its commandant.

After *Svante Nilsson* (*Sture*) had occupied Oslo with a Swedish force (May 1503) he advanced into Vestfold, killed Mattis Alsen, captured Tønsberghus which he burnt to the ground, and plundered the town. This tragic story was entered (1550) in *Codex Tunsbergensis:* 'Year 1503 Tønsberghus was destroyed by the Swedes and the town plundered.' The castle was never again rebuilt.

* See 'East Norway and its Frontier.'

The Reformation

During the reigns of Christian II and Frederik I (1515–33) Tønsberg was deprived of many of its ecclestiastical institutions, viz.: St. Michael's Church, the leper hospital at Gunnarsbø, and the Abbey of St. Olav with that of the Franciscans. In 1524 *Erik Ugerup*, a Danish noble who had married a daughter of Fru Inger til Austraat, was granted Tønsberg len and took up residence at Sem kongsgaard.

During the struggle of Archbishop Olav Engelbrektsson to uphold the independence of Norway he had all Vestfold on his side. Then, in the very year of establishment of the Reformation (1536) the entire town of Tønsberg was burnt to the ground. The stone walls of five out of its seven churches were demolished to provide dwellings for post-Reformation citizens, and only those of St. Laurence and Maria stood as monuments of the observance of the Old Faith. Tønsberg was deserted by its citizens until a decree was issued (1538) ordering their return to their old hearths, and so the town began a new life.

Culture in the Middle Ages

All the while that Tønsberg was a royal residence and fortress town it was the scene of numerous national assemblies and ecclesiastical conferences. The *Union of Kalmar* (1397) put an end to the use of Tønsberg for important gatherings, when it was reduced to a mere provincial centre.

Codex Tunsbergensis (*ca.* 1550) contains the MS. of the Church laws, and the provincial secular law (Borgartingslov). Tønsberg's town law (bylov or farmannslov) was committed to script (*ca.* 1320) together with decrees of King Haakon V. This MS. remained in Tønsberg until *ca.* 1600, and found its way to the Royal Library at Copenhagen in 1769. An outstanding manuscript which provides evidence that procedure in the Courts was excellent, it is a cultural memorial of great value. Another law codex from late 1300's is preserved in the Royal Library at Stockholm. *Borgarting* is first mentioned in 1224 as being held at Sarpsborg—it was the 'parliament' for Vestfold, Grenafylki,

4. Ulefos Manor House

Herregården, Larvik

5. The whaling fleet at Sandefjord

Svend Foyn

Vingulmark and Ranrike. Tønsberg had its own lagmann (man-of-law) in 1266, and perhaps even earlier.

The wealthy abbey of St. Olav owned vast properties in Vestfold, with Sem kongsgaard as centre of its estates. The monks of that Premonstratensian Order were the pillars of such culture as existed until the arival of *Queen Blanche* who introduced (*ca.* 1340) refined French taste in architecture and furnishings to backward Vestfold.

Trade in Late Middle Ages

Rostock—which acquired the status of a 'city' early in thirteenth century—was granted privileges at Tønsberg by Haakon V in 1318. Those Hansa traders were styled 'Wieck-fahrer,' and to them Magnus VI continued to grant—and often to retract—privileges. Haakon VI did his best to secure internal trade for Norwegian nationals, but war resulted from his attempts and after an armistice (1369) the Rostock traders returned. A peace was concluded in 1376, but differences in the interpretation of its terms occurred in the year following.

The notorious pirates known as 'vitaliner' * had their lairs at Rostock and Wismar. When those two cities broke away from the Hansa Union they made a separate peace with Erik of Pommern (1430). The ports around Oslofjord did not suffer from the depredations of the 'vitaliner' to the extent that Bergen did, and so in South Norway the Rostockers were received with open arms as late as 1440. Then war broke out and heavy taxation was imposed on the Germans.

Indignation ran high among south Norwegians when Christoffer of Bayern granted privileges to Rostock and Wismar; yet it seems that the King had a subtle motive in pacifying the Rostockers, since it gave him a freer hand to deal with the troublesome Lübeckers at Bergen. Matters did not improve for Tønsberg merchants under Christian I, who confirmed Rostock's privileges in 1477—it was during the reign of that king that the cities of Mecklenburg attained the zenith of their power in the north.

* See 'West Norway and its Fjords.'

Christian II abolished all Hansa privileges (1508), but as he ran short of cash he made a fresh grant at his wedding feast (1513), and Rostock was again in the ascendant. Christian III reversed this (1538) and gave full support to citizens of Tønsberg so that Rostock's position became extremely weak. After the Reformation the Dutch stepped in to oust Rostock and Wismar from their pre-eminent position in the trade of Vestfold, and under the terms of the Odense Recess (1560) the Germans were all but eliminated from Denmark–Norway.

From earliest times timber export had been carried on at numerous loading-places in Vestfold fylke. *Snekkestad* was mentioned in a letter of Edward I (*ca.* 1280)—*Sandefjord* appears in Sverre's Saga (*ca.* 1190)—Melsomvik in Stokke (*ca.* 1390).

By the 1320's the Germans were trading direct between Tønsberg and Kings Lynn, and were well on the way to become lords of commerce in Vestfold.

CHAPTER IV

FROM REFORMATION TO ABSOLUTE MONARCHY (1537–1661)

The Last Century of Tønsberg 'Len'

THE devastating town fire of 1536 destroyed Tønsberg at the very moment that all-embracing ecclesiastical reforms swept away the traditional institutions of the Old Faith. Moreover, that 'spiritual' upheaval coincided with a colossal increase in timber export due to the employment of water-driven saw-mills.

The considerable properties belonging to St. Olav's abbey came into the hands of a Danish nobleman *Erik Ugerup* who was made 'lensherre' of Tønsberg. An uncultured man, he lived at Auli (Ulen) in *Sem* with his wife—a daughter of Fru Inger til Austraat. That celebrated lady from Trøndelag wrote a letter that survives, dated from 'Royal Sem 1539.' Erik Ugerup was dispossessed (1542) by an infinitely more attractive Danish noble, *Bent Bille:* a paper feud continued between them for some years, which gives a good insight into conditions in Vestfold during their era. Bent Bille lived at Auli until his death in 1571, when he was buried in Sem church; his grave has survived.

On Bille's demise the vast properties of ancient St. Olav's abbey came to the family of *Lange*, who were destined to play vital roles in the fylke for many a year to come. The first Lange came from Skaane and lived for forty years at *Falkensten* until his death (1612). His son *Gunde Lange* then took over, and in his old age was 'colonel-in-command' on the Swedish frontier during the 'Hannibal War.' It was while Gunde Lange was lord of Sem in 1626 that he engaged as secretary a remarkable Dane from Haderslev named *Anders Madsen* (1609–70)—of whom more anon. Gunde Lange handed over his 'len' (1633) to Admiral *Ove Gedde*—a sailor who had led an expedition to the East Indies and acquired the sovereignty of Tranquebar for his king.

He settled down at Sem, and extended his activities over Brunla, Numedal and Eiker—becoming controller of the Kongsberg mines in 1630. He commanded the Norwegian coastal flotilla at the engagement of Listdyp, and retired to Denmark (1650) leaving behind an excellent reputation.

The days of 'feudalism' were numbered, and with the assumption of *absolute power* by Frederik III in 1661 a new administrative system was introduced. Under the name of *Brunla Amt* the 'len' of Tønsberg was united to that of Brunla—an ancient district whose 'tingplace' was at Tjølling and which embraced the south-west part of Vestfold Fylke.

The Last of Brunla 'Len'

A young Dane named *Ivar Jenssøn* arrived in Norway in the 1520's to enter the service of Mogens Gyldenstjerne—Frederik I's commandant at Akershus. He was granted the Convent of Gimsøy (Skien) when the 'Reformation' seized the properties of the Church, but again embraced the Old Faith and joined up with Christian II. This caused him to lose all his grants, but before the wealthy Karen (sister of Knut Alvsson) of Grefsheim (Hamar) died (1536) she gave him an estate in Sandar (near Sandefjord). Then for some unknown reason he acquired the family name of *Jernskjegg* (Ironbeard—once the nickname of that famous old Trøndelag chief who was killed by Olav Tryggvesson during sacrifices at Maere).

Ivar Jernskjegg began operations at the fortunate moment when waterpowered saw-mills were initiated. And so where the River *Laagen* from Numedal runs into salt water, and a second river—the *Farris*—slightly to the westward also has its outlet, he acquired properties at the south end of Farrievannet. These key positions have formed the heart of *Fritzøe Verk* down to our own times. Several fosses below Farrisvannet provided the power, and here Ivar Jenssøn began operating saw-mills in 1539. He continued to buy up estates, including that of Brunla, and became 'principal of the King's mines in Norway.' Having died in 1570 he was buried in *Hedrum* church in the Jernskjegg family vault.

His son Peder carried on the mills and was visited at Fritzøe by Bishop Jens Nilssøn (1593) whilst a huge feast was in progress. He describes a stately stone mansion, standing on the west side of the Jomfru peninsula at south end of Farrisvannet. The Jernskjeggs petered out in 1615, but their gravestones in Hedrum church recall the tales of the founders of Fritzøe Verk and of the city of *Larvik*.

Gunde Lange (see p. 51) (1595–1647) acquired Fritzøe Verk in 1623, after marrying a granddaughter of Fru Inger til Austraat. His finances went awry and in 1634 he mortgaged Fritzøe and Fossesholm to the Crown.

His son, *Niels Lange* (*ca.* 1600–52) took over Fritzøe, which during the 'Hannibal War' (1643–45) was at the height of its prosperity. When Hannibal Sehested had to submit his accounts for audit they were found to be in woeful disorder, and as 'Treasurer for Norway' Niels Lange was responsible: he was deprived of most of his properties. He died a broken man in 1652, and, in the following year his widow—a daughter of Admiral Ove Gedde—passed through a night of terror when a flood broke the dam at Farrisvannet and the old mansion slipped into the storm of waters and disappeared. Although they had acquired vast properties in Vestfold, the sole memorial of the *Lange* family is *Langestrand*, the western portion of the town of Larvik at the mouth of the River Farris. It was here that Lange's ships loaded their timber cargoes in those far-off days before the old mansion was swept away by the flood. It had grown into a 'ladested' in the time of the last Jernskjegg, who had five saw-mills working on the Farris before 1593. He it was who acquired all the land on which Larvik now stands, and founded the ironworks at Fritzøe.

The New Bourgeois Leaders of Tønsberg

The economic life of Tønsberg during the seventeenth century was controlled and impelled by three remarkable citizens. The earliest was *Iver Nielsen* who sailed his own ship to Rostock (1611) and later made several voyages to Scotland and England. After his death in 1622 the widow continued to swell the fortune he had amassed. The second merchant prince was *Anbjørn*

Lauritsen, who became the leading figure in the 1640's and died in 1657 a very wealthy man.

The most outstanding figure was, however, *Anders Madsen*, a Dane who was born at Haderslev where he received an excellent education, and was engaged as accountant by Gunde Lange when lord of Sem in 1626. Before long he was acting as Lange's attorney for all public activities in Tønsberg 'len,' in which city he took citizenship in 1636. He became its borgermester two years later, at the age of 29, and continued to hold that post until 1663. Anders married into the family of *Coldevin*, and his wife's brother Jørgen—the second generation of that Danish family in Norway—worked together with him to dominate civic life in Tønsberg, and economic affairs in Vestfold, for a period of some thirty years.

It was Anders Madsen's initiative which began the flotation of felled timber from far up the rivers, and he opened branches of his firm at many ladesteder, e.g. Larvik, Holmestrand and—most important of all—at Strømsø (Drammen). He routed his own ships to Holland, England, France and Spain, and acquired immense wealth from saw-mills and timber export. Like his predecessor, Iver Nielsen, he made loans to peasants, nobles and the Crown, and when payments defaulted he acquired ownership of vast holdings and of such famous estates as Herre-Skjelbrei. Anders was principal creditor when Niels Lange's widow lost her all in the flood which swept away the old house at Fritzøe (1653), and that property also fell into his hands.

When his end came in 1670 people maintained that he surely sold his soul to the Devil—else he could not have amassed such wealth from a poverty-stricken Vestfold. He grabbed everything he could put his hands on between 1640 and 1670, and the bulk of the citizens were reduced to low circumstances and faded out under the intolerable yoke he forced on their shoulders. Borgermester for twenty-five years, with his brother-in-law Jørgen Coldevin as his obedient tool, it is very doubtful whether his labours were beneficial to Vestfold. Worn out by business worries Anders Madsen died in 1670 and was buried in St. Laurence church. His widow continued to run his vast undertakings until her death in 1698. He built a house in Tønsberg (1630) which was known until recently as *Madsegaarden*—named after his son-in-law, Mads Gregersen. It was rebuilt in 1807 but burned to the ground in 1898, when its site was used to build the Victoria Hotel.

Anders' sons adopted the family name of *de Tønsberg*, one of whom, Mathias (1638–1705), was amtmann of Buskerud fylke. Another, Stig, accompanied Gyldenløve to London on his Embassy to Charles II. *Stig de Tønsberg* resided at Borgestad as a wealthy ironmaster, and was buried at Skien. Many leading families in Norway and Denmark—notably the Wedel-Jarlsbergs and Løvenskiolds—trace their descent from Anders Madsen.

National Events in Vestfold (1537–1661)

Tønsberg played no major role during the long century, but was most fortunately spared destruction when the Swedes invaded (1567) and burnt the town of Skien. They did, however, on that occasion burn Erik Ugerup's former house at Auli (once the 'Home Farm' of St. Olav abbey's estates). Tønsberg no doubt owed its survival to the splendid defence put up by Malte Hansen.

When Princess Anna was driven back to Flekkerø by rough seas (1589) King James VI of Scotland hastened to that port, and thence via Langesund to Sandefjord. There he spent the night at the rectory called 'Florents'—whose priest, the famous Peder Vemundsen, had named it after the City of Florence where he had studied (1573). King James moved on to Tønsberg, where only two churches had survived the Great Fire of 1536—St. Laurence and Maria—and it was at the former that he listened to his own chaplain (16th November, 1589) preach from the text 'The Lord is my Shepherd' in the Scottish tongue. James left his five ships in Tønsberg and rode through the forests to Oslo where he was married on 23rd November. A week later the honeymoon couple returned to Tønsberg with a following of fifty; as snow had meanwhile fallen they drove in sledges. From Tønsberg they took the land route to Copenhagen where they arrived at the end January 1590, and made their return to their Scottish kingdom in the spring.

Bishop *Jens Nilssøn* of Oslo has recorded in his diary some vivid descriptions of social activities in Vestfold around the year 1600. They plainly show that whenever there was 'fun' to be had the aristocratic families had not the least objection to amuse themselves among the bourgeoisie—baptisms and weddings were especially very mixed affairs. The tombstone in Hedrum church to Peder Jernskjegg and his wife Fru Margrete Breide, preserved the memory of two of the nobility who organized 'frolics' at their Fritzøe mansion. Other places where fun and games were held were Auli, Aker, Falkensten and Fosnes.

Under the influence of 'Kloster-Lasse'* there was a strong leaning to the Old Faith among clerics in Vestfold during the seventeenth century. Three sons of *Rasmus Hjorth*, the Archdeacon of St. Laurence, Tønsberg, showed their papistical leanings too openly and were haled before a 'herredag' in Skien, where Christian IV in person and the Bishop of Oslo extracted confessions. All three were deprived of their offices and exiled. Vestfold was a centre for the so-called '*acta jesuitica*' in early seventeenth century, but the harsh edicts of Christian IV (1624) finally uprooted all opposition to the Lutheran Confession. The clergy at St. Laurence leant to the Roman Confession, those at Maria to the Lutheran.

Communications continued in a woeful state and Vestfold was roadless. *Skelljastenssund* (now Kanalen) which Haakon IV had dredged to shorten the sea-passage to Oslo, was silted up again during the Middle Ages—Knut Alvssøn sank a ship in it during his investment of Tønsberghus (1502).

Trade Following the Reformation (1537–1661)

The introduction of water saw-mills (*ca.* 1539) brought many Dutch vessels to the small fjords, whose skippers bought direct from the peasants. The citizens of Tønsberg then roused themselves and acted as middlemen, since Tønsberg was unfavourably situated for the timber trade owing to the paucity of coastal forests and lack of floating facilities from the great rivers. Drammenselven and Laagen were the principal timber rivers,

* See 'East Norway and its Frontier.'

and since a royal decree gave Tønsberg trading privileges—which they shared with other towns—along the coast between Gothenburg and Ana Sira, there was great scope for initiative among its citizens.

Its two most prosperous ladesteder were *Strømsø* and *Holmestrand;* the former waged a lengthy dispute with what is today its twin member of the City of Drammen, viz.: *Bragernes*. The latter was a limb of Oslo whilst *Strømsø* occupied a similar position under Tønsberg.

Sandefjord had exported timber since Saga times, whereas *Larvik* was not mentioned until the 1500's, and then in connexion with the Jernskjeggs.

Trading activities at Tønsberg dwindled so greatly after the death of *Anders Madsen* (1670) that King Christian V ordered his viceroy to move the town and its people to Hølen, near Larvik. Although this edict could not be carried out, yet it shows to what depths Tønsberg had sunk, though the idea no doubt emanated from Gyldenløve, who was extremely jealous of Anders Madsen. Between the Reformation and the introduction of absolute monarchy (1661) Danish and Holstein nobles had played an active part in Vestfold. Then a new aristocracy grew up and the old families were swept away—often under tragic circumstances. New men with commercial acumen—such giants as Anders Madsen and Nils Toller—stepped into their shoes.

The two 'counties' of Vestfold were established, and the families of Jernskjegg and Lange became but memories.

CHAPTER V

THE TALE OF NORWAY'S TWO COUNTIES

The County of Griffenfeldt (Jarlsberg)

WITH the advent of absolute monarchy, the royal dictator's powerful statesmen angled for 'noble' estates in Norway, from which they might take their titles and rule over their petty 'kingdoms' in semi-regal state.

In the summer of 1671, King Christian V ennobled his famous Chancellor *Peder Schumacher*, and granted him the deeds of such properties as had belonged to the Chapter of Tønsberg, together with the 'kongsgaard' of Sem. This 'county' was styled *Griffenfeldt*, and from it the great man took his title: the ancient mansion of 'Kongs-Sem' was renamed 'Griffenfeldt-gaard.' Two years later that great statesman was appointed 'amtmann' in Tønsberg, though without the obligation of dwelling within that 'amt.' Following his disgrace in 1676 the entire plan for a semi-feudal 'County of Griffenfeldt' fell to the ground, and he himself began his term of eighteen years' imprisonment at Munkholmen, Trondheim. Thus it came about that Peder Schumacher never enjoyed his small personal kingdom, and the Crown again took over, whilst the name of the mansion reverted to 'Kongs-Sem.'

When *Ulrik Frederik Gyldenløve* bought the property and noble rights in 1678, he became proprietor of a vertitable 'principality' embracing all Vestfold—then known as Tønsberg County. He renamed the mansion of Kongs-Sem to that it bears today, viz.: *Jarlsberg*, for it seems that he adopted the English title 'earl' to denote his own status in the ranks of the nobility. When the old mansion burnt to the ground (1682) Glydenløve lost interest: being in need of cash and heavily in debt to Wedel's son, he sold 'Jarlsberg County' to Baron *Gustav Wilhelm von Wedel* (1641–1717) a member of an old Holstein family. A deeply religious man, Wedel spent large sums restoring the ancient stone churches in his 'county' and partly rebuilt Jarlsberg—the east and west wings are his work. Since the first two 'Counts of Wedel-Jarlsberg' did not settle down there permanently its completion was long delayed—indeed not until Christian VI and his Queen Sophie Magdalena paid a visit in 1733 was the grand mansion finished and furnished.

When the Wedels entered into possession of the 'county' (1683) the Crown retained the City of Tønsberg under its own jurisdiction, and also detached the 'ladesteder' of Holmestrand and Strømsø from the original 'County of Griffenfeldt.'

The illustrious family of *Wedel-Jarlsberg* remained 'Danish' until *Frederik Christian Otto* (1718–76)—the third Wedel to own Jarlsberg—took over at the age of twenty. He was the first Wedel to speak Norwegian as his mother tongue: he completed the mansion and much of his work in the south wing survives. He laid out his park on the model of Versailles: the avenues known as 'Count's allé' and 'Field-Marshal's allé' are reminders of his days—the latter leads to the little wood 'Gullkronen,' wherein an area was consecrated as the family burial place in the 1860's.

In 1750 the reigning count was compelled to sell a portion of his county because of debts incurred from deficits at the unlucky ironworks of Konnerud, near Strømsø. His brother, who was living in Denmark, blamed him abusively for that sale—the latter was founder of a branch which numbered the celebrated Count Fritz Wedel-Jarlsberg among its scions.

The fourth of the line, *Frederik Anton the second* (1748–1811), was born at Jarlsberg, and became ambassador in London. His wife was imbued with the notions of the French Revolution and deserted her 'conservative' husband; their two sons, Herman and Ferdinand, followed her example soon after. Herman took his mother's part and maligned his father in print—an action which led to more than a little condemnation from sections of posterity.

This *Herman Wedel-Jarlsberg* (1779–1840) was born at Montpellier, and spent many of his early years in France, Italy and England. He was to become the greatest Wedel of them all, and remains a national figure. His outlook on life was deeply influenced by his youthful years in France and England, whilst absolutism and bad administration in Denmark made him unsympathetic to that country. Owing to his high birth and fortunate marriage to *Karen Anker*, daughter of Peder Anker of Bogstad, he occupied both socially and economically a position which was unique in Norway. Although he and his wife spent most of their lives at Bogstad and were thought to have had no love for Jarlsberg, yet it was he who rebuilt (1813) part of the south wing and the 'empire' façade that survives.

Count Herman's greatest work in Vestfold lay in the sphere of agriculture, since he appointed as manager of his estates (1812) the philologue *Jacob Sverdrup*. Of that venture Jens Kraft wrote (1822): 'Since 1812 a new era has dawned in agriculture owing to improvements in method on the Jarlsberg estates.' Those practices were adopted as models for farming methods all over Norway.

Count Herman played a major role in national affairs during the struggle for independence.* In 1836 he was appointed 'statt-holder,' though by that time he was worn-out and crippled by rheumatism. He died at Wiesbaden (1840), and Wergeland wrote in the local paper: 'Norway deeply mourns the loss of its statt-holder, Count Wedel-Jarlsberg. A man of Napoleonic drive, courageous, noble, indefatigable, of great foresight, gifted, unambitious and a lover of mankind.' His funeral at Jarlsberg was a national event.

Count *Peder Wedel-Jarlsberg* (1809–93) was the last holder of an hereditary title in Norway. He married a daughter of Carsten Anker, was a sailor and greatly respected. His brother Harald of Baerums Verk had also been to sea—the two had much in common. In his days Hans Gude, Theodor Kjerulf and Camilla Collett were frequently guests at Jarlsberg—the latter gives a lively account of life there in her sketch 'At an ancient noble seat' (1861).

Karl Wedel-Jarlsberg, who died in 1946, devotedly restored the famous house during the 1930's, and brought many secrets to

* See 'East Norway and its Frontier.'

light. Jarlsberg maintained its own school and system of poor-relief for all employed on the Sem estates; these institutions were not superseded until 1933.

An atmosphere from the distant past and a sense of great traditions pervade the buildings to an extent that is uncommon in Norway, and its dignified rooms house a wealth of treasures, including works by Moroni, Opie, Romney, Hoppner, etc., as also a precious collection of the productions of Norwegian silver-smiths. The 'Riddersal' (Knights Hall) is indeed a joy to twentieth century eyes.

The ancient church of *Sem* (*ca.* 1080)—the very church in which Harald Gille walked barefoot across nine ploughshares—is now the parish church.

The County of Laurvig (*Larvik*)

The other mansion in Vestfold which became the centre of a 'county' is that now known as *Treschow-Fritzøe*—and the 'county' was *Laurvig*.

Ulrik Frederik Gyldenløve—an illegitimate son of Frederik III and the popular viceroy of Norway for nearly forty years—wanted to assemble a number of contiguous properties in his ownership so as to found a 'county' over which he might rule in semi-regal state. His fancy drew him to the estates of the noble family of *Lange* lying in Brunla, together with Fritzøe and its saw-mills and ironworks. The Langes were at that time heavily in debt, and although jomfru Ida Lange of *Falkensten* put up a stiff fight to retain their patriarchal estates, it was only a matter of time before they fell into the melting-pot.

Gyldenløve's schemes concerning Larvik induced him to represent to Copenhagen that Tønsberg was a town in decay, and that its citizens should be forcibly removed to Larviksfjord. In this matter, however, he went ahead too fast, and met with such stubborn resistance from the good people of Tønsberg that they were able to demonstrate that their town was not 'an almost deserted city' as he had represented it to be. Therefore Tønsberg remained independent of the new 'county,' which was established for the benefit of Gyldenløve by a decree of 29th September, 1671, and in the year that followed all links between the town and county were severed. The result was that Tønsberg lost its ancient ladested *Sandefjord*, which together with Tjølling, Hedrum, Brunlanes, and Tjøme all formed part of the County of Laurvig.

Ulrik Frederik Gyldenløve (1638–1704) continued the activities at the mouth of the Farris which the Lange family had carried on. *Fritzøe Verk* had begun smelting in 1642 with ore brought from the Arendal district, and cannon were cast as well as bar-iron and stoves. It was at that period the largest industrial works in Norway, and the surrounding forests were denuded of charcoal. Gyldenløve owned all the land up the river Laagen, and by 1703 four-fifths of the former Brunla 'len' were within the county limits. It was that first Gyldenløve who demolished the old Fritzøe (Fresjar) house, and built (1675) the mansion at Larvik which stands today and is yet known as 'Herregaarden.'

Two years later Gyldenløve left his command in Baahuslen (1677) to marry his third wife—the seventeen-year-old Antoinette Augusta of Oldenborg—at Larvik.

The great house was largely rebuilt and extended in the 1730's, and in more recent years has served many purposes—official residence, town hall, ball-room and school. When it was restored a few years ago it was found possible to revert to its original plan, and it stands as a unique example of *régence wooden* architecture in Norway.

Gyldenløve's son, *Ferdinand Anton Danneskiold-Laurvigen*, built the 'Hospital'—a fine old dwelling which is today the 'gamlehjem' (old peoples' home). He owned no fewer than seventeen saw-mills in outlying districts as well as seven at Fritzøe—even the mines at Braastad near Arendal were drawn in under his ironworks. As late as 1781 Fritzøe was producing twice as much iron as the output of Ulefos. That first Danneskiold-Laurvigen was a pietist and, like his son Ludvig, lived mostly in Denmark. When the latter died childless (1754) his younger brother, *Christian Conrad*, took over and made up for the respectability of his two predecessors by a scandalous way of life. He brazenly abducted an actress, jomfru Rose, and when tongues wagged in Copenhagen he had the effrontery in the presence of the King to deny having done so. His monarch imposed a fine and also exiled him to his Norwegian county. He returned to Denmark some years later, where he ran into debt and was obliged to hurriedly retreat to Larvik. There he found consolation in the embraces of Ingeborg Akeleye, the wife of *Herman Løvenskiold* of Fossum. After the latter had divorced her she continued to live with her Conrad in a small house at Hedrum. Owing to his defiance of the marriage laws he was known as 'the wicked count'—the twentieth century would surely not be so severe?

The Gyldenløve line died out with Christian Conrad, the only member of that family who lived in Norway. After lengthy legal proceedings Count *Christian Ahlefeldt-Laurvigen* took possession—to be followed by his son Frederik. The family life of both was disreputable, the younger Frederik being morally depraved. In 1805 the State bought him out.

The intention of the 'national planners' was that charcoal from the vast forests and the iron ore from Arendal should be diverted to Kongsberg, and iron smelting replace the dwindling silver production there. But Kongsberg's iron works never paid, and at the Treaty of Kiel in 1814 a secret clause was inserted that 'the county should remain the property of His Danish Majesty.' Three years later during the difficult period of inflation the King sold out to buyers who could not complete the contract, and several legal proceedings began regarding 'county' rights. In 1820 the town of Larvik bought the section within their town limits, excepting *Langestrand* which was a portion of Fritzøe.

William Frederik Treschow, from Denmark, acquired all that remained of the Gyldenløve properties. His ancestor had been a wealthy merchant and citizen of Naestved, in Sjaelland, whose patronymic was Treskomager (wooden-clog-maker), but his own paternal relations for three generations had filled posts in Norway, his father being a Counsellor who was ennobled in 1812. William Frederik left Denmark on taking possession and made contact with the great agricultural pioneer Jacob Sverdrup, of Semb (near Horten), who had married his sister. Treschow had too many connexions in Denmark to be able to abandon them, and Sverdrup made an excellent manager until his death in 1841. Treschow tided over the economic storm which brought most other industrialists to bankruptcy, and after 1842 world markets opened wide for a great expansion of iron and forestry products; thus was the estate of Fritzøe built up again.

Michael Treschow (1814–1901) lived at Fritzøe from 1839, and in 1845 he bought Froland Verk in Aust-Agder. Trade in their own schooners began in the 1840's: iron to, and corn from Denmark, timber to France and England with coal as return cargo, and finally iron and emigrants to U.S.A., bringing back rice. By 1850 there was intense activity—one great contract being the chain bridge over Sarpsfossen, a construction which no other firm in Norway could undertake. In 1865 iron export slowed up, and in 1868 the smelting ceased after being conducted for two and a half centuries.

Michael's son *Fritz*—known as 'kammerherren'—was 100 per cent. a Norwegian and a great art collector. In 1877 the name was changed to *Treschow-Fritzøe* and mechanized wood products became the main line of activity. He had no sons so it passed to a nephew Fritz Michael (born 1879) whose firm built power-stations which provided current to most of Vestfold. On the property grows the largest beech-forest in Norway.

When Treschow bought the properties the mansion at Larvik was not included, so in 1860 he built a mansion on the high plateau to the west of Langestrand. It is not in the taste of today, but contains a large collection of Scandinavian art from late nineteenth century.

It is a long cry from the days of the Jernskjeggs to modern Treschow-Fritzøe, but the kernel in the complex of production has ever been the works around Farris river. In the western part of the harbour of Larvik stand the firm's quays and warehouses; up at Farris are the timber booms, and scattered around are the various residences, including the old Fresjar which slipped into the flood waters (1653). The mansion at Larvik from Gyldenløve's days—the little manager's home from the Lange period—and finally modern *Fritzøehus*. Still on the banks of the Laagen and Farris flourish the vast forests which are the *fons et origo* of all.

6. Cast iron portrait of King Frederik V
from Holden iron foundry

Right : Beechwood at Larvik

7. Altar and organ at Kongsberg Church

CHAPTER VI

THE CITY OF TØNSBERG THROUGH THREE CENTURIES (1661–1940)

NEW administrative organs were introduced by Frederik III when he assumed absolute powers (1661), and most Norwegian towns were granted new charters when they passed from 'lensherre' control to that of bureaucrats. Tønsberg got hers on 30th July, 1662, but such contentious matters as its interests in Agder and the ladested of Strømsø were passed by and left unsettled.

The last part of the seventeenth century brought good times for Tønsberg because much of her trade being with Denmark she did not feel the paralysing effects of the British Navigation Acts (1651 and 1661). Those measures hamstrung the shipping of the Dutch and led to hostilities breaking out between the two Great Powers—England and Holland. Norway was drawn into that war in 1666, in which year the amtmann held a Council at Tønsberg to proclaim the decree that all Englishmen were to be arrested and their goods sequestrated. When the Gyldenløve War broke out (1675) Tønsberg's trade with Denmark was seriously affected, but between 1688 and the Peace of Ryswick (1697) Norwegian shipping enjoyed a series of wonderful years until the outbreak of the Great Northern War (1709) which led to its ruin and great poverty and distress throughout Vestfold.

Tønsberg was honoured by five visits of Dano-Norwegian kings—Christian IV in 1598, Christian V in 1685 accompanied by Ulrik Fredrik Gyldenløve, and by Frederik IV in 1704. The latter dined at Jarlsberg and slept at *Madsegaarden* as guest of Mads Gregersen from whom the house received its name: he was a nephew of Anders Madsen and took over the latter's business in the name of the widow in 1670. Mads Gregersen (born 1651—died childless in 1733) was in his last year when he welcomed Christian VI and his numerous following to his

'Madsegaarden' in 1733—the second monarch he entertained there. Frederik V came on 9th July, 1749, and Crown Prince Frederik (VI) sailed in from Drammen in 1788. The numerous descendants of Anders Madsen trace their descent from Mads Gregersen's brother Anders.

* * * * *

After the devastating fire of 1536 no fresh alarming outbreak of that curse of timber cities occurred until 1683, in which year the church of *St. Laurence* was yet a second time left with nought but its grey walls upright. The citizens restored it immediately, and after undergoing several restorations it was again reduced to bare walls in a great fire of 1736. Forty years later the clergy started a movement for its demolition, and after the tower was pulled down in 1804 all services ceased. Strangely enough it was from the Treasury in Copenhagen that suggestions came (1809) for its preservation, and in their report they state the reason for their attitude to be due to the fact that 'it is an outstanding building from past times.' Alas! the local pundits had made up their minds, and demolition began in the following year. There then remained but one church out of the seven which had at one time graced Tønsberg, viz.: *Maria church*—a bell from whose tower, dated 1536, hangs in the present cathedral.

The attitude of the city fathers to their two mediæval churches was deplorable, and posterity cannot do other than condemn them for their wanton destruction. The present cathedral was built on the site of St. Laurence in 1858, and five years later came the turn of Maria for destruction by the local 'vandals'—although the influential *Svend Foyn* led the opposition to its demolition. The City Council required a plot for the erection of a 'Raadhus'—so what could be more suitable than that of their sole remaining *mediæval* church? Some of Maria's furnishings were transferred to the 'Cathedral'—including the magnificent pulpit of native workmenship from 1621—whilst the remainder were disposed of to the highest bidder! Then down came the old church of Maria in which their ancestors had uttered their prayers, for divine help in this life and the next, during more than seven hundred and fifty years. The day the demolition was taken in hand several of Svend Foyn's employees marched to his house (Storgaten 54). Their spokesman said: 'We know that the captain is opposed to the destruction of Maria church and we wish to know whether he would like us to stop the work now going on? You have only to say the word and you can be sure we shall remove the men who are now demolishing it.' Svend Foyn had, however, to refuse their offer—though later on he came to bitterly regret not having exercised his authority over them, for the loss of such a rich Tønsberg tradition cut him to the quick. It was an irreplaceable loss which everyone deplores today. Svend Foyn vowed he would never enter the raadhus—the cause of such a piece of sacrilege—and when King Oscar paid Tønsberg a visit the grand old man declined to attend him within.

In view of the great antiquity of Tønsberg it was but natural that some interest in its history was evinced during the eighteenth century during which Jens Müller wrote 'Tønsbergs Beskrivelse' (*ca.* 1750). The ruins all around kept fantasy alive, and induced its inhabitants to site within their city boundaries the events told and retold in their folk-legends: e.g. they claimed that Axel and Valborg had made love on their Slottsfjellet. Peder Clausson wrote 'Jarlsbergs Beskrivelse' in 1743, and such was the pride of all Norway in the glorious past of Tønsberg that when a Norwegian University was mooted there were many—including Christen Pram—who wished to see it established there. Even Nicolai Wergeland favoured it at one time—and very nearly succeeded in his efforts there—but was unable to abandon his own Kristiansand.

Mary Wollstonecraft spent three weeks in Tønsberg during the summer of 1795, when she paid many visits to Slottsfjellet. She tells us that on her rambles around the old castle ruins she seldom met a soul, and there she often lay down to sleep on the soft moss that covered the ancient stones. She paints an interesting picture of life in the homes of the bourgeoisie, and remarked on the extreme slowness of the servants serving food, and of the colossal amounts consumed. She was struck by the excessive number of decayed teeth which the young girls were unable to disguise, and noted that she found the same distressing conditions among Swedish lassies.

It was in 1797 that *Hans Nielsen Hauge* began his evangelism in the 'counties,' where he found a few 'God-fearing people' who were remnants of the followers of two earlier Moravian priests. Except around Ramnes he made little impression in Vestfold, where the local priests received his evangelism with 'silent contempt.' Although they themselves were preaching to empty churches, they continued that attitude for many years, until in 1852 a considerable Christian Revival took place.

It was this spiritual awakening which necessitated the provision of a new and larger church than the ancient Maria, and so the present 'cathedral' arose in 1858. The salutary influence of Svend Foyn was mainly responsible for solving the long and bitter disputes which had raged among Tønsberg's parishioners. Possessed of an active social conscience and no friend of mere doctrine, he took the initiative to draw young men together who had a 'call' for social service, educational work, sick visiting, and calls on old people. The pastors regained their influence and actively supported Svend Foyn when he provided funds for missions—both at home and abroad.

The Struggle for Independence

As in the remainder of Norway the outbreak of war with England brought disaster to Tønsberg (1807). As is usual on these occasions there was a witch hunt for traitors and spies, and when two merchants named Holst had their letters intercepted to English business friends they were arrested—but cleared their reputations sufficiently to get off with a nominal fine.

The loss of eleven of its ships in 1809 was a severe blow to Tønsberg—they were seized by English privateers whilst trading to Denmark. Such losses were annual recurrences until 1814, and impoverished Tønsberg. That town lay, however, outside the coastal districts where Norwegian privateers were fitted out.

Towards the close of 1809 the King granted permits to purchase English licences, and several fully laden vessels set off to

England with timber—to return with holds full of corn; hence 1810–12 were comparatively good years. All trade ceased again in 1813 when yet another period of poverty set in, which resulted in a form of State Bankruptcy before the year was old.

When the National Assembly met at Eidsvoll the representative of Tønsberg, *Carl Stoltenberg*, was firmly on the side of Christian Magnus Falsen, and opposed to Count Wedel-Jarlsberg's pro-Swedish policy. On his return to Tønsberg (29th May, 1814) he was received with salutes and garguantuan feasts, the principal one being given by Mathias Foyn at Teie.

Vestfold after Napoleon

There was complete stagnation in Tønsberg after Waterloo (1815): the economics of Vestfold for several decades make a woeful story. Larvik and Holmestrand—two former ladesteder subordinated to Tønsberg—were completely independent by 1817, and even Aasgaardstrand came under Holmestrand town, all rivals to Tønsberg. The saltworks at *Valløy*, which had been founded in 1739 and flourished until the slump in 1807, met difficulties after 1819 and decay set in. Many distilleries were established and drunkenness was rampant, whilst bankruptcies were the order of the day.

Shipping, which had ever provided the main source of livelihood for the people of Tønsberg, was restricted to voyages to Danish ports until well into the 1820's. Then the famous Tønsberg family of *Walløe* fitted out six armed ships to sail to Spain and the Mediterranean, which used their armaments to keep at bay the pirates off Algiers. Shipping was so much on the upgrade that Wergeland could write in the 1840's: 'The sails of Tønsberg ships are scattered over the oceans like a shower of stars in the mirror of the seas.'

There was great excitement when the first steamship to visit Norway—'Constitutionen'—called at Valløy. At that time most vessels lay at Traela or Jersøy owing to the difficulty of approach to Tønsberg—at Jersøy there was an excellent harbour where ships laid up for the winter in closely packed ranks. In 1835 a private company dredged 'Stenkanalen' to a depth of 7 feet in order to provide a short cut to Jersøy and Christiania, instead of using Vrengen channel.

On the outbreak of the Franco-Prussian War in 1870, local sentiment was entirely on the side of France and the 'tricolour' flew on Slottsfjellet and from many public buildings.

Tønsberg's greatest day of rejoicing came on the 23rd June, 1871, on which day it was decided to celebrate the one thousandth anniversary of the foundation of the town. After Divine Service everybody swarmed up to Slottsfjellet to sing the famous verse which Bjørnson had specially composed—'Du mere end tusend Aar gamle By' (Thou ancient town, more than one thousand years old). Bjørnson then declaimed his oration, and walked down from Slottsfjellet in the company of his bitterest political opponent, Ludvig Daae; even fierce political wrangles were forgotten in the joy of a great tradition.

Seals, Whales, and Svend Foyn

The greatest benefactor that Tønsberg and Vestfold have ever possessed was *Svend Foyn*, who was born at Tønsberg in 1809, and died there on 30th November, 1894. Its leading citizen in the 1770's and 1780's was Svend's forbear, Samuel Foyn (died 1786), when his business passed to his son Andreas. Svend's uncle Mathias Foyn rebuilt *Teie* in 1803, and was the richest man in Tønsberg through many decades (see pp. 69 and 75). The family had originated in *Foynland*, on Nøtterøy. When Svend's father was drowned at sea (1813) his mother was left with five small children, all under twelve, and there was great poverty in the Foyn home. Svend somehow made his way to England to learn the language, and later to Paris where he studied French for six months: when he was whaling off the coast of Finnmark many years later he was able to converse freely with the Czar Alexander III who was voyaging in those parts. A 'skipper' at the age of twenty-four he married in 1839, but three years later they separated by mutual agreement as being temperamentally unsuited. In that same year (1842) his mother died, so bereft of mother, wife and home, he determined to make a fortune and set off for the coast of Finnmark to initiate an entirely new source of national wealth.

Ever since *ca.* 1820 the people of North Norway had been hunting *seal*, but only in a small way, and Svend Foyn was the first to embark on an independent arctic hunting expedition (1847). His crew were loud in their grumbles at the meagre dividend that fell to their share, but Foyn himself was satisfied that with perseverance such ventures would pay and he applied to the State for a subsidy or loan, only to meet with a refusal. He then borrowed from relations and went north with a vessel appropriately named 'Haabet' (The Hope) (1848), when he fell in with innumerable seal. That spring he caught no fewer than six thousand fat seal which he took to Altona for sale; this scale of success was repeated over a series of years.

Other Tønsberg skippers followed suit in the 1850's, with the result that a 'Vestfold' sealing fleet based on Tønsberg brought considerable wealth into the little town. Sandefjord followed Tønsberg's lead in 1855, and it was obvious that Svend Foyn had opened up fields of activity which greatly enriched Norway.

The arctic seal has its young around 23rd March each year with surprising regularity. Until the young seal are five days old their mother never leaves them, and the dog-seal remains close at hand all that while. If the cold is intense he keeps a blow-hole opened by bobbing up and down uninterruptedly throughout the twenty-four hours so that the mother can pass up and down to her young. These regular habits of the seal were so exploited by the hunters that the species faced extermination, and so a law was enacted creating a *close season* until 3rd April, after which seal-hunting ceased to be such an attractive operation.

The hunters turned to the *bottle-nosed whale* during the 1870's, but not until the next decade did the new venture become a major activity. Yet seal-hunting continued well after 1880, and slowly but surely the seal was as good as exterminated over wide stretches of the Arctic Ocean. The crews signed on at a low wage, but their share was one-sixth of net dividend: in three months' sealing they could earn more than in twelve months on ordinary trading voyages. Although the work was by no means free from danger, their health statistics show they suffered little. The seal oil was disposed of to home and foreign markets; the skins went mostly to the London auctions.

Norwegians have hunted whales spasmodically from remote times. It was, however, the depression in agriculture and industry during mid-nineteenth century which led up to Vestfold's immense contribution to whaling and shipping after the 1840's. There was an urgent call for an explosive harpoon which shattered the whale on striking, and so prevented the monster from making off with the catching tackle before death came. Svend Foyn may have borrowed many ideas for his explosive harpoon from that of an Englishman named Welch, who produced one in 1867, i.e. three years before Foyn's, which was a definite improvement.

Foyn began to employ steam vessels as early as 1863, and during the 1870's the annual catch averaged some forty whales. These he processed in his own boiling plant at Vadsø in Finnmark, which Jonas Lie called 'a vast installation.'

An enterprising German went to Finnmark and enticed away many of Foyn's trained crews (1872) to take service with him. Foyn maintained that such competition would ruin all hopes of Norway deriving national wealth from whaling, and sought the assistance of the authorities. They granted Foyn (1873) sole patent rights for ten years for all his inventions, and he retained a virtual monopoly in whaling as late as 1883. He was the uncrowned king of Finnmark whence came much wealth to Vestfold, and Jonas Lie sang his praises in verse and prose. Tønsberg erected a statue close to the Cathedral, where he was a regular worshipper until death came for him in 1894.

Foyn also traded in other commodities and frequently made journeys to the Gulf of Bothnia to purchase timber and to fix freights at rates very much to his own advantage—he became owner of a considerable fleet. When England revoked her Navigation Acts (1849) Tønsberg shipping prospered exceedingly; shipbuilding also enjoyed great prosperity during the Crimean War. Many Vestfold ships took supplies to the British fleet in the Baltic and were used as transports from the Crimea to Constantinople. After that, emigrant traffic to the New World swelled to immense proportions during the 1860's: certain Vestfold shipowners travelled far and wide throughout Norway persuading struggling peasants to take passage in their ships to distant lands 'where the strange roads go down.'

The Last Century in Vestfold

The story of Vestfold during the last one hundred years is that of shipping and antarctic whaling. When mineral oil was struck in Pennsylvania (1859) the initiative of Vestfold shipowners laid the foundations for that vast fleet of 'tankers' which is the pride of Norway today. It was Captain *Even Tollefsen* of Tønsberg who found a solution to the question of bulk carriage of oil when his ship carried the first cargo from Philadelphia to Rouen. Tollefsen was born on Nøtterøy (1841), and thirty years later he converted the first three sailing ships that ever sailed the seas as 'tankers'. Before 1880 steam was replacing sail, and in due course the considerable Norwegian sailing fleet was converted into a still larger steam fleet.

Among the many shipping lines which have originated in Vestfold not one spans the oceans to the extent that *Wilhelmsens* do. Their saga began with a ship named 'Talabot'—the forerunner of the many which transformed the company's fleet from sail to steam. It was in 1886 that young Halfdan Wilhelmsen returned to Tønsberg at the age of twenty-three from a period of study of methods of shipbrokers in many ports, including London. Three years later he returned to England to purchase the 'Talabot,' a vessel of 805 tons and Wilhelmsens first steamer. By 1939 that company's fleet numbered fifty-two ships of 315,000 tons and it is now the largest shipping company in Norway. Conditions during the First World War caused the company to transfer its Head Office to Oslo (1917): its ships are, however, still registered at Tønsberg, which prides itself on being the mother city of the fleet. When the firm celebrates its centenary in 1961 the festivities will be held in Tønsberg.

* * * * *

Whaling was freed from restrictions by the Government in 1883 and many new companies began to operate. This led to such a reduction in whale population in the Arctic Ocean that the fishermen of Finnmark succeeded in compelling the Government to prohibit the catching or processing of whales in North Norway.

Svend Foyn when an old man had foreseen that new fields must be sought, and sent a ship to the *Antarctic* to prospect in 1893. Progress at Tønsberg was now surpassed by that at *Sandefjord*, where Christen Christensen and his son Lars (born 1884) became the pioneers in Antarctic whaling; in 1912 Sandefjord possessed twenty-seven hunting stations whilst Tønsberg had no more than ten.

By the 1930's whaling ships had increased both in number and in size, the effect on life in Vestfold from the colossal profits accruing being immense. In 1931 just over 5,000 'whalers' mustered for the season from Sandefjord, more than 4,oco from Tønsberg and about 600 from Larvik. A grand total of 10,549 sailed away to the Antarctic that year, 7,946 of whom were natives of Vestfold.

* * * * *

When the one thousandth anniversary of the foundation of Tønsberg was celebrated in 1871 (see p. 70) a wooden tower (erected 1856) stood on the site of 'Teglkastellet,' but it burnt down in 1874. The present stone structure, which is such a landmark for miles around, was erected in 1888.

Three years later a committee was formed to debate the deepening of 'Kanalen Stenen' (Skjelljaastenssund), and by 1896 it had been dredged to a depth of 21 feet. On 15th May that same year the ship 'Norway' of the Grangemouth Salvesen Line was saluted at Husøy as she steamed into the ancient waterway which Haakon IV had deepened to open a short route to the east—now a new canal with great possibilities.

The two artistic 'lions' of Vestfold are the artists Hans Heyerdahl and *Edvard Munch*—both of them lived at Aasgaardstrand where the latter's house is now a museum. The father of 'Expressionism' had a violent quarrel with the champion of the classical school in Norway, von Ditten. So heated did their hostility become, that under the influence of drink the two protagonists came to blows and the police had to be called in (1904). The leading Vestfold sculptor, Carl E. Paulsen, was born at Tønsberg. He has been called 'the polar sculptor' because he made a speciality of modelling arctic explorers. That is why Tønsberg has his statue of Roald Amundsen, who himself had no connexion with the town.

The good folk of Tønsberg gave an enthusiastic welcome to King Haakon VII and Queen Maud when, together with Crown Prince Olav, they paid their first visit to Slottsfjellet on 1st August, 1906, whilst staying at Jarlsberg.

On the outbreak of war in 1914, panic reigned in Tønsberg with a rush on the banks and a frantic urge to dispose of Treasury Notes; small coins were collected and an acute dearth of change resulted. Prices continued to rise, and after 1915 pseudo-prosperity produced the 'sin' of avarice which spread throughout the land in a violent wave of materialism. The slump in 1920 brought many tragedies—which distressing state of affairs lasted until 1926. Not until the early 1930's did the 'depression' begin to fade away.

Tønsberg Today—and Tomorrow?

The City Fathers of Tønsberg set a fine example to all communities by their happy blending of material progress with affection and respect for ancient traditions. The ruins on Slottsfjellet are carefully preserved from any extraneous ugliness, whilst the little that remains of the foundations of St. Olav's abbey church in Storgaten will shortly be enclosed in a small public garden—although this will necessitate the demolition of a dwelling house. Mathias Foyn's 150-year-old house at *Teie* has been carefully restored to provide a forum for purposes of higher education, whilst its ancient basement from the days of the Roman Catholic bishops of Oslo remains more or less undisturbed. A 'fylkes-museum' preserves countless relics from Vestfold's long-ago, and also houses a 'whale museum' which gives a picture of the methods by which the seamen of Tønsberg have so enriched their city. Gunnarsbø mansion stands 'en-parked' as a memorial of an early Wilhelmsen—and also perhaps to recall the tragic inmates of the leper hospital that for long stood on its site. The open squares of the town are being enriched with mosaics and graceful statues from Italy; it is obvious that a sense of beauty and love of art in its most pleasing forms are impelling the ruling spirits in Tønsberg city. It is a happy thought for an Englishman to know that their town of Sunderland has been adopted by Tønsberg—and that their respective coats-of-arms hang in each others City Halls. This link is strengthened by the annual visit of twenty-five Sunderland school children to the homes of the kind and generous people of Tønsberg. Now there is a possibility that Belgian Namur will reforge its link with Tønsberg which was first joined by its Queen Blanche 600 years ago.

In 1948 the Government decided to divide the Diocese of Oslo by creating one to embrace the fylker of Vestfold, Buskerud and Telemark. The three provincial capitals were asked what financial support they were prepared to give to the new bishopric, and since *Tønsberg* assured the largest sum it became the Cathedral City of the new Diocese.

What of the future? Will the whales in the South Atlantic be exterminated in the near future, and so deprive Tønsberg of its gold-mines? This nightmare does not deter the City Council from planning a transfer of its main harbour from the west end of 'Kanalen' to its eastern entrance at Træla where deep draught ships can moor. One feels sure that even if the whale disappears, such enterprising citizens as those of Tønsberg will develop other sources of wealth to maintain their present high standard of living—and their priceless international deeds of goodwill and kindness.

CHAPTER VII

A PERAMBULATION OF VESTFOLD FYLKE

The Peninsula of Brunlanes

WHEN making a historical pilgrimage through Vestfold Fylke, it is fitting to begin at its south-western extremity where Olav II (the Saint) wrote the first paragraph of a new volume of the 'History of Norway' at the Battle of Nesjar in *Helgeroa* (Holyrood) Bay. The countless ghosts of bronze-age chieftains lying in their barrows at *Mølen* hard by, must surely have hovered anxiously around on that Palm Sunday in 1016, and scuttled away into oblivion when the 'Champion of Christianity' had won his decisive victory. The dedication to St. Olav of the nearby church of *Tanum* is a reminder of the stakes he won on that great day.

Throughout the Middle Ages the peninsula of Brunlanes played an important role: its mansion of *Brunla* was for two centuries the home of Norwegian and Danish noblemen—notably the all-powerful Henrik Krummedike (*ca.* 1500). It was absorbed into the Fritzøe estates by the Jernkjeggs (*ca.* 1600): not until 1840 did the present Brunla gaard revive its aristocratic traditions when it was occupied for several years by a Wedel-Jarlsberg. The Church of the peninsula was *Tanum* (*ca.* 1200), which has among its ancient furnishings a font sculptured by a 'gotlending' (*ca.* 1230).

From the picturesque little harbour of *Nevlunghavn*—or 'Havna' as it is locally known—the artists Fritz Thaulow and Munthe have left us charming vignettes upon their canvases. Here is an ancient pilot-station which must often have provided the base of operations for that almost legendary pilot *Ulabrand*, who came from the coastal village of Ula at the entrance to Sandefjordsfjord. Ulabrand—who was drowned in 1881, aged sixty-seven—was the embodiment of all the virtues possessed by that fine body of coastal-pilots who guided ships around the coast of Vestfold.

Stavern is an aristocratic town with a great naval tradition. When Christian V was visiting Gyldenløve at his county residence of Laurvig (Larvik), he ordered the construction of a base here, and a fort was built for its protection (1689). Stavern first came into prominence during the Great Northern War, when *Tordenskiold* was a frequent visitor: it was here that he brought in as prize the Swedish privateer 'Svenska Vapen,' which had struck to his own 'Løvendals Gallei,' and now from Vigeland's statue his gaze is ever over Stavern. Frederik V decreed in 1750 that a naval station be built on Citadeløya—under the name of *Frederiksværn*. The Naval Academy was established here in 1817, and was not transferred to Horten until 1864; then Stavern began to decay, and was abandoned in 1896. Some picturesque buildings survive—notably the Garrison church (1756)—to recall the days when it was the 'Portsmouth' of Norway. On a prominent headland here stands *Minnehallen*, a pyramid to commemorate the seamen who perished in the First World War. That great novelist *Jonas Lie* and his wife Thomasine lie together in the churchyard.

Much of the story of *Larvik* has already been told (see p. 61 *et seq.*). It has ever been a point of departure for Jutland, and in recent times has become the terminal harbour for the Larvik-Frederikshavn ferry which links the two closely related countries. Above the town towers the fine beech forest which is Larvik's pride—yet another link between it and Denmark, 'the land of beeches.'

The Home of the Whaling Fleet

Tjølling is the most ancient centre in Vestfold, since it occupies the site of the mart of *Skiringsal* where Frisian traders brought goods from lands afar before and during the Viking Age (see p. 21). Sigurd Jorsalfar built (*ca.* 1120) the church which still stands, and 'Brunla ting' was held in its churchyard as recently as 1557.

At the head of Sandefjordsfjord lies the port of *Sandefjord*, the largest whaling centre in the World. During the fourteenth century there was a small timber export, yet as recently as 1830 it had no more than seven hundred inhabitants. Whaling in the South Atlantic was pioneered at the turn of the century by two Sandefjord men—Chr. Christensen and C. A. Larsen. This development induced Great Britain and Norway to annex much of the Antarctic continent, and to limit licences for whaling—a regulation which prevented excessive slaughter for twenty years, after which period other freebooting nations began to operate. Immense wealth has accrued to all Vestfold, and especially to the six thousand people who now have their habitat in Sandefjord, which also houses an International Statistical Bureau to keep track of destruction of whales and to formulate plans for conservation of the species.

At the western entrance to the broad Oslofjord lie the twin islands of *Færder* with their famous lighthouse, and opposite lies *Tjøme* point—known as 'World's End.' Christian Krogh painted several seascapes off Tjøme; at a later date Jean Heiberg worked at Grepa on that island.

The Western Shore of Oslofjord

The two large islands of Tjøme and Nøtterøy are divided by the channel of *Vrengen;* with its bridge from 1932. Between Nøtterøy and Tønsberg city runs 'kanalen,' which was called in mediæval times 'Skjeljastensund' (the sound with a dividing stone).

Some 3 km. north-westward of Tønsberg lies the ancient estate of *Aker*, which has been immortalized by Sigrid Undset in 'Kristen Lavransdatter.' She describes an incident here at the time that Erling Vidkunnsson (see p. 42) owned Aker (*ca.* 1329), whilst he was the leading figure in Norway after the male line of Sverre had died out (1319). Erling often resided at Tønsberghus, but it is not known whether he ever used his house at Aker. The Krummedikes—father and son—owned the estate from 1450 to 1530; it then passed to the Jernskjeggs. Laurence Foyn bought it (1875) and carried on ship-owning and seal-fishery with his famous brother Svend Foyn. The oldest part of the present building is from 1812—it lies prettily situated at the head of an ash avenue.

When passing the barrow at *Slagen* within which the *Oseberg* ship was buried, one is amazed that it lies so far from salt water, with no more than a trickling stream as a connecting link. The answer seems to be that the river up which the Oseberg ship was floated has brought down masses of alluvial deposit during the intervening eleven hundred years.

Aasgaardstrand has a long history as a timber-loading place: for long it has been but a seaside resort which has housed some celebrated artists, including Edvard Munch and Hans Heyerdahl (see p. 74). Nearby stands the stone church of *Borre*, which was erected soon after the introduction of Christianity close to the mausoleum of the 'ynglinge' kings, and perhaps on the site of the temple at which they sacrificed in their day. The barrows lie in a thicket which is now a National Park—peaceful reminders of the turbulent vikings from eleven hundred years ago.

The ancient estate of *Semb* lies most picturesquely around the Lake of Borrevatn. It was the experimental farm of *Jacob Sverdrup*, who founded an Agricutural School here in 1825. A century later the father of Norsk Hydro—the great industrialist *Sam Eyde* (1866–1940)—retired to Semb, bought up surrounding properties and initiated the latest agricultural practices as a model for all Norway. Fears arose among those with a narrow outlook that his modern methods would put the small farmer out of business, and that other industrial magnates would acquire too much 'odel' land. Sam Eyde had many successes and not a few disappointments, but had the satisfaction to leave a flourishing property to his son Sigurd, when he died at Aasgaardstrand in 1940 and was buried in Borre Churchyard. Alas, the old mansion at Semb has gone: the present house is from 1910.

One year after Norway obtained its independence, a commission decided to establish the headquarters of the Norwegian Navy at *Horten*, which was at that time merely a farm and ferry station. So for one hundred years this place has existed for the Navy, but strategic necessity now makes it imperative that the naval base be moved to a fjord on the west coast—hence the future of Horten is problematic. The town is well on the way to absorb the ancient noble estate of *Falkensten* (see p. 51) whose ancient mansion of the Langes was burnt in 1770 and rebuilt nearer the seashore. There was a well near here in the very-long-ago at which numerous miracles occurred, and so a primitive chapel of *Løvøy* was built, remote from all habitation, and dedicated to Saints Hallvard and Martin. It seems to be a fact that 'King Philip of East Norway' died on the little Løvøy peninsula, whither he had come for cure (1217)—it was around St. Hans Eve (Midsummer Eve) that the miraculous powers were exerted at their utmost. Services continued to be held here long after the chapel had become a ruin: indeed, as late as the nineteenth century the miracle-working water was drawn from the chapel well. Bishop Jens Nilssøn wrote at end of the sixteenth century that the building had for long been derelict, and the owner obtained a permit (1720) to rebuild—though that structure had but a short life. Yet again it was rebuilt in 1930. *Falkensten* estate came into the hands of an inventor during the eighteenth century who designed—on the model of an English plough—'The Falkensten Plough,' which was taken into general use throughout Norway after 1771.

Further north up the coast lies the ancient loading-place of *Holmestrand*. It possesses an interesting mansion with a heavy façade (from *ca.* 1750) called *Gausen*. The artist Harriet Backer lived here, whilst the writer Nils Kjaer and the painter Hans Gude have left us many peeps at byegone Holmestrand.

The Interior of Vestfold

Most of the history in the fylke has been made on its sea-coast—for its upland is of very limited area. St. Olav's abbey in Tønsberg owned most of it until the Reformation, when the Crown took possession. The costly Swedish wars of mid-seventeenth century led to the sale of many estates.

Melsom in Stokke came to Vincents Bildt (1649) who soon unloaded it on the wealthy Nils Toller of Christiania; it is now the agricultural school for the fylke. *Fosnes*, also in Stokke, came to *Preben von Ahnen* (1649), who played a great role in the story of Nordland fylke.* The descendants of that old junker through

* See 'North Norway.'

the female line continued to dwell at Fosnes and farm its land as late as 1850.

At *Høyjord* survives the only stave church in all Vestfold. It is from *ca.* 1250, and has a weathervane of gilded bronze which emblazons a coat of arms that may be that of Duke Skule. In the parish lay the famous estate of *Herre-Skjelbrei* with its legends of 'Mindre Alv.'

At Ramnes were fought the two battles of *Re* during the Civil War.

The historical gem of northern Vestfold is, however, the charming mansion at *Eidsfoss*, which stands on the narrow isthmus, dividing Bergsvannet from Eikeren. It came into the possession of that remarkable Dane and mayor of Tønsberg *Anders Madsen* (1609–70). Its most interesting owner was, however, General Caspar Herman *Hausmann* (1653–1718)—a son of Margaret Pape who had been Frederik III's mistress. This stepbrother of Ulrik Frederik Gyldenløve was dismissed from the command of the troops in Norway during the Great Northern War. He inherited vast properties from his wife, Karen Toller, whose father was from Haderslev, and also from his mother-in-law who was a daughter of Anders Madsen, likewise a Haderslevian.

Eidsfoss had been drawn into the 'County of Jarlsberg,' and thus it came about that in 1697 Count Wedel-Jarlsberg issued an edict that General Hausmann should select a spot in the parish of Sande to open up smelting works. A circumference was delimited, and 279 estates passed over to the ironworks, which were to erect saw-mills, brickworks, etc. There was water-power in plenty, and charcoal in unlimited quantities from the vast forests around, but ore was present only in small deposits. Transport was a difficult problem—whether northward through Eikeren to Drammenselva, or across the divide to Sande.

Hausmann speculated heavily during the golden age of the Great Northern War in many forms of industrial and commercial endeavour. He lived for the most part in the bishop's palace in old Oslo, and on his death (1718) his most efficient widow kept the works running until their son, Frederik

Ferdinand Hausmann (1693–1757) took over in 1742. For some reason unknown he began selling off parts of his properties—perhaps life at Eidsfoss was too dull for him. Under his successor named Rasch (1774) Eidsfoss Verk was one of the largest iron producers in Norway.

Its golden days were, however, to be under Peder *von Cappelen* of Strømsø (Drammen, 1763–1837)—a son of Diderik von Cappelen of Skien who had founded the family fortunes. He bought up Konnerud works (1801) which had been a drain on the Counts of Jarlsberg, and in 1824 acquired the Kongsberg ironworks which had likewise never paid a dividend. He operated the three smelting works as one concern, and the stoves of Eidsfoss won a great reputation for artistic elegance. Peder was the sole considerable citizen of Drammen who withstood the slump of *ca.* 1821—he was a cultured man who lived mostly at Austad on the boundary of Drammen town. They kept open house at Eidsfoss during the summers, and there he died in 1837.

When her two children—both daughters—died, Fru Maja and her grandchildren migrated to the famous Moravian centre at Christiansfeldt (South Jutland) where one of the granddaughters was prioress.

All Norway's ironworks began to fade out in the 1850s, and that wild speculator from Odal, John Collett Bredesen, wrecked the former Cappelen firm. A forced sale brought Eidsfoss to an English company, whose Norwegian adviser was John Crowe, the famous British consul-general in Christiania. When William Pare, the English chairman, died at Eidsfoss in 1873 the works returned to Norwegian ownership. They are still in full working till this day, though its products have changed their character.

The mansion at Eidsfoss dates mainly from Hausmann days (*ca.* 1700)—a perfect period piece—and the so-called 'white room' is still furnished with antiques from the time of its erection. It lies in a world of its own, and remote from main lines of traffic and tourist routes.

PART II

BUSKERUD

CHAPTER VIII

BUSKERUD FYLKE

IN the dawn of history there was a petty kingdom in *Ringerike* in northern Buskerud which was conquered by Halvdan Svarte (*ca.* 830). When that mighty chieftain of Vestfold died, his body was quartered and one portion—the head—brought to Ringerike. Does this grim relic lie in 'Halvdanshaugen' (?) on the estate of Stein. That the 'head' was brought here seems to show that Halvdan Svarte had a particular affection for Ringerike, although later generations knew him as a *Vestfold* king; possibly it was within that 'kingdom' his 'heart' was laid to rest, among his forbears at Borre? Halvdan Svarte's second wife, Ragnhild, was a daughter of Sigurd Hjort of Ringerike, a clever woman whose sleep was interrupted by fantastic dreams of might and power. She became the mother of *Harald Fairhair*.

Ringerike did not, however, attain its flowering period until it had witnessed the birth of little *Olav* (*ca.* 995)—son of *Harald Grenske* and later to be canonized as *St. Olav*. Aasta, his mother, fled from Skien after the murder of her husband, Harald Grenske (a great-grandson of Harald Fairhair) by *Sigrid Storraade*, Queen of the Svear (see p. 105).

It seems more than probable that St. Olav was born in the district of Hole near Bønsnes Church, and the saga states that the great event occurred in the house of Gudbrand Kula, who was Aasta's uncle. Shortly after little Olav's entry into this world his mother married the chieftain of Hole named *Sigurd Syr*, who brought the boy up. They had a boy of their own named Harald —later to become so famous as King *Harald Haardraade*—and thus it came about that the two mightiest kings of Norway in the early Middle Ages played together as children around the cape where Bønsnes juts out into beautiful Tyrifjord.

Olav and Harald went on their various ways, the former

to return to Bønsnes in the autumn of 1015, when the saga tells the story of his home-coming. Servants ran into the 'hall' with the news of his arrival, and told his mother the tale of his recent victories on the Norwegian coast. Aasta gathered together her men and women and made them dress up in their finest attire. Then she rearranged the 'hall' with extra benches, cloth-hangings and straw on the floor. Two men were sent to Sigurd Syr who was working in the fields, with his best clothes and gilt saddle, as well as his horse's bridle which was adorned with precious stones. Aasta sent four men round the neighbourhood to summon the leading peasants—and to those who had no 'best' clothes she lent her husband's and her own. 'King' Sigurd Syr, out in the fields, dressed himself in a blue tunic and breeches of the same colour, a grey cloak and broad-brimmed grey hat, veil over his face and in his hand a staff with a silver crook, to which was attached a silver ring.

The saga then gives a long account of what chatter passed between Queen Aasta's messengers and Sigurd Syr, who then changed his attire again by clothing himself in silks with a scarlet cloak and gilded helmet when he mounted his horse. Then Sigurd Syr rode up to the farm where Olav's standard was waving in the breeze, and the young prodigal was surrounded with 120 men all in magnificent raiment. When Sigurd Syr bid Olav welcome and invited him to the drinking-feast, Aasta stepped forward and kissed her son, begged him to consider all that was hers to be his own, and that she tendered her services to him. King Olav returned thanks for her offer and then Aasta took his hand and led him to the dais. Sigurd Syr sent his men about their various businesses and then joined wife and stepson on the dais, where they were feasted with abundance.

King Olav had not been long at the Hall before he let his mother and Sigurd know it was his intention to reclaim his real inheritance at the point of the sword, for which purpose he asked the help of his relatives. Aasta at once promised him all he asked, but Sigurd Syr was rather hesitant for a while. Eventually he gave Olav his assurance he would use all his influence with the 'Oppland' kings on Olav's behalf. Thus supported, Olav began his royal progress through the Opplands, and met with no opposition until he reached Trøndelag and its 'Earls of Lade.'

Little is known about the details of Harald *Haardraade's* childhood at Bønsnes, except a story that young Olav was unable to rouse any feeling of fear in his infant stepbrother Harald, whilst he terrified Harald's two brothers with gruesome stories; but such fanciful tales were almost certainly the inventions of the saga writer who was 'wise after the event,' i.e. wrote up Harald's fearless character in later life as having been evidenced when he was but a little boy.

The Church of Bønsnes is said to have been built by St. Olav, but the date of the oldest part of the present structure cannot be earlier than 1075. Pilgrims probably came this way to dally where the saint had lived—certain it is that Ringerike provided a well-trodden highway from the sea to the Opplands of Hadeland, Toten, etc.—and Storelva was navigable for many miles above modern Drammen.

* * * * *

Ringerike owns a wealth of historical tradition in both legend and saga. Archæological finds from the Roman and Migration periods (A.D. 200–600) have been numerous, but surprisingly little has been unearthed from the Viking Age (A.D. 600–800). An exception is a remarkable 'find' made in 1943 at Haugsbygd in Norderhov, where a chieftain was buried with a gilded helmet beside his body. It is the first time a helmet from so late as the Viking Age has been found in Norway, its date being early in the tenth century. It is, however, for the particular style of ornamentation on wood, stone and metal which was introduced into Norway when Olav II established Christianity there, that the name of 'Ringerike' has acquired world-wide fame. In this form of art called '*Ringerikestyle*' the prime motifs were taken from the plant world, and were quite new to Norwegian decoration. Previously heads and limbs of animals had provided the usual motif, but with the first breath of Christianity came representation of leaves—sometimes surrounding figures of animals. Arabic and English influence is clearly traceable, but Norwegian artists left their own impress on their fascinating works of art. The beautiful bronze weathervane at Heggen church in Modum is an outstanding example of this.

Some thirteen years after the death of St. Olav at Stiklestad the legend of *St. Hallvard* had its origin. In *ca.* 1043 a chivalrous gentleman of Lier had put up a defence for an unknown pregnant woman whom he had never seen, and her persecutors killed Hallvard and threw his body into Drammensfjord, with a millstone round his neck. Yet despite that heavy 'sinker' Hallvard floated to the surface, with green leaves sprouting from the willow wands that served to attach the stone to his neck. The new town of Oslo needed a local saint and at once adopted the knightly Hallvard—indeed his image still stares out from the City's coat of arms, complete with millstone attached.

The long century of civil war passed by without great effect upon modern Buskerud—it had no coastline from which marauding nautical thugs had an opportunity to devastate the peaceful peasantry. One intriguing figure was thrown up from Ringerike in the person of *Alv Erlingsson* of Tornberg (Tanberg). He belonged to an old family whose members had played a great role in national history, though the contribution of this Alv to his country was far from beneficial, since he had no political importance but was a mere adventurer. In the troubled years following the death of Magnus V when two little boys nominally shared the throne, Alv Erlingsson fished deeply in troubled waters and ingratiated himself with the Queen Mother Ingeborg, who secured his appointment as 'Earl of Norway' in 1285. He travelled to England as ambassador to Edward I to try to raise money, but met with very little success in that venture. He returned home in August 1286, and in the year following his protectress Queen Ingeborg died. Alv, in his office of 'protector of the Realm of Norway,' addressed a violent protest to the Scottish King's seneschal when he impounded some Norwegian vessels at the behest of the Hansa cities. He ended his protest: '. . . if you do not cease such high-handed actions against Norway you shall know she is not yet so feeble that she cannot cut off your spurs.' When Queen Ingeborg died his influence was over, and at the head of a band of cut-throats he burst into Oslo, burnt down part of the town and murdered Duke Haakon's commandant. His strange action is believed to have been due to a secret connexion with King Magnus of Sweden—to which country he fled when outlawed in Norway. After three years in an abbey there he recommenced his piratical life, and ravished the coasts of Denmark in 1290. On that foray he was caught at Helsingborg, and killed after mutilation, his remains being brought to Tønsberg for burial. His family died out with his end, but an assortment of legends and songs have lived on in folk memory both in Norway and Denmark concerning 'Mindre Alv'—who was so called because he was such a small fellow but did some exciting things. His latin title was 'comes de Saresburgh' (knight of Sarpsborg) and he probably lived in the island of Isegarn where modern Fredrikstad stands.

CHAPTER IX

THE EASTERN DISTRICT

TODAY the usual approach to Buskerud is by Drammensveien, across Paradisbakken (the Paradise Hill) to the district of *Lier*. This was not always so, since until 1660 there was no road leading from Oslo that ran further east than Asker, and when Bishop Jens Nilsson visited Drammen at the close of the sixteenth century he found it advisable to row round Hurumlandet owing to the evil state of the land tracks.

Lier lies on the north shore of Drammensfjord and has a coastline with salt water thereon which is about 5 km. in length. It runs north as far as Holsfjord, which is the southern arm of Tyrifjord, from which its own river—Lierse lva—runs for *ca.* 12 miles to the fjord. Legend is busy here, and even whispers that Ragnar Lodbrok built his vessels here? During the Civil War King Sverre fought some skirmishes in Lier, and 'birchlegs,' 'bagler' and' ribbunger' all brought trouble to the district. In a far later century the defending Norwegian forces withdrew from Oslo (1716) to Gjellebek to stem Karl XII's further advance eastwards, and their position was so strong that Karl detached a force of dragoons to outflank Gjellebek by encircling Nordmarka via Norderhov, where Anna Colbjørnsdatter worked her wiles so successfully.

Across Paradisbakken and through Lier 'plankekjøring' (deal driving) was carried on similar to that in Romerike,* but not on so large a scale, to the quays of Drammen for export. Also a frequent sight were the landaus and closed carriages which kept up communication between Oslo and Drammen until the Randsfjord railway was opened in 1868; this put Lier outside the traffic for the few years that elapsed before the opening of the Oslo-Drammen railway in 1872.

Drammen in history is the amalgamation of two towns of

* See 'East Norway.'

Bragernes which was a limb of Oslo, and Strømsø which occupied a similar position in regard to Tønsberg. The latter's suburb of Tangen was also drawn in to the City of Drammen when its two moieties amalgamated in 1811. Export of timber is known to have existed as early as 1340, but dwelling here did not arise in numbers until mid-sixteenth century. Then Bragernes was frequented by Danes bringing corn, whilst Strømsø was the port for English, Dutch and Germans. Christian IV decreed (1632) that citizens of Bragernes were to remove to his precious city of Christiania, but to no avail. Then in 1657 dwellers in Strømsø were ordered to pay Christiania rates—despite the fact that the ladested lay within Tønsberg len. When absolute monarchy was established a petition from both sections of Drammen was sent to Frederik III begging to be granted freedom from Christiania, and that if the combined 'town' was granted this request it might be named 'Frederikstrøm.' Nothing came of this, however, and not until 1715 were 'town charters' granted to the several cities of Bragernes and Strømsø. They were amalgamated in 1811 and named *Drammen.* As late as 1789 citizens of Bragernes opposed the suggestion for union on the grounds that Strømsø might succeed in attracting the entire upland trade. Now Drammen has become Norway's principal pulp export harbour which passes across the quays at Tangen, and it seems a long cry since Samuel Pepys wrote in his diary of 23rd June, 1662, that he had just been down to see a dozen ships at London quays which had come in from Drammen and two other Norwegian ports loaded with deals.

West of Drammen lies the district of *Eiker* and its great lake of Eikeren, which together with Fiskumvannet is some 20 miles in length. It is but natural that a district so near the sea and semi-feudal Vestfold should possess rich traditions from the long-ago. An outstanding find was made at Nedre Hon in Eiker in 1834—numerous golden ornaments and coins of Byzantine, Frankish and Anglo-Saxon origins. These told a story of trade and cultural connexions with East and West Europe and were surely the treasure of some temple to a god of olden times—probably dating from ninth century.

Eiker housed the most famous glass factory in all Norway at

Nøstetangen, a part of the glebe of Eiker rectory. The factory began working in 1741. At first it produced utilitarian as well as ornamental glass, but from 1748, when Aas took over that activity, Nøstetangen concentrated on making the finest glass products. The magnificent chandeliers in Kongsberg church are among these, and others are now museum pieces. The demand for fuel for Nøstetangen was so great that the entire works were moved in 1778 to Hurdal, where timber was at hand in more generous amounts.

Modum must be regarded as the centre of Buskerud fylke, for here lay the mansion of Buskerud, which gave its name to the fylke when it was formed in 1918 and broken off ancient Akershus Amt. The estate of Buskerud was in the ownership of Colletts for 120 years, until they sold it out of the family in 1883.

In the districts of Eiker and Modum some large estates existed in the seventeenth and eighteenth centuries. Peder Hansen Litle had owned *Fossesholm* in Eiker (1540), which was later the residence of *Hannibal Sehested.* On his fall in 1651 it became Crown Lands, and later the estate was divided up among timber-exporters of Drammen, while part of it was parcelled out among the peasantry during the eighteenth century. At *Sem* lived the lensherre for Eiker, Admiral Ove Gedde, a splendid building with a long façade which was built in the hope it would house a king. Christian IV came here in 1635 when on his way to inspect Kongsberg. Sem has vanished, but Fossesholm still stands with its earliest part some two centuries old. Jørgen Cappelen commissioned the artist E. G. Tunsmarck to decorate a series of rooms with scenes from daily life at the time.

Forestry has ever been the mainstay of the districts. In a report of 1823 it was stated: 'the peasants of Modum and Eiker have little regard for agriculture,' and in the 1770's a factory for production of blaafarge began, which by 1840 was employing more than 1,000 workmen. Then aniline dyes were invented and that spelt the ruin of Modum's factory which ceased operations in 1898. Wood products opened a new era when a German, Gottlob Keller, invented a method of mechanical pulping, and *ca.* 1900 paper factories opened here.

Medicinal water was found at Modum in 1840, which brought many sufferers to 'St. Olav's bath.' The Red Cross Society bought out the baths in 1940, and it is still the 'Harrogate' of Norway.

Dramselva is the name for the mighty river that flows out of Tyrifjord through Modum to reach salt water in Drammensfjord. Between the two southern arms of Tyrifjord and Drammen lies *Finnemarka*, a desolate area with conifers and heathland which is almost uninhabited except along its boundaries.

* * * * *

Around the northern shores of Tyrifjord is the ancient Kingdom of *Ringerike*, which is bounded to the east by the mountain plateau of *Krokskogen*, rising abruptly from the eastern shore of Tyrifjord. To the eastward of Krokskogene's vidde lies the neighbouring district of Baerum—and indeed the outlying parts of Oslo City. To ascend the vidde the ancient path was that of the famous *Krokkleiva* rising almost sheer from Sundvollen. It was here that Jørgen Moe wrote his famous description of Ringerike. The rise is *ca.* 1,000 feet and the famous view-points Dronningen and Kongen give vistas of all Ringerike and away to the distant mountains. There is an aerial railway nowadays—so tourists are spared the dangers and discomfort of negotiating the hazardous Krokkleiva, which was one of the old roads linking Christiania with Ringerike.

In the district of *Hole* lies the ancient estate of *Stein*—approached by an avenue of century-old balsam poplars from the main road.

Snorre repeated the age-old legend that Halvdan Svarte's head was buried in 'Halvdanshaugen' at Stein, where some funeral furnishings were found in the barrow. Several saga-characters are mentioned as living in Ringerike, including Sigurd Syr (father of Harald Haardraade), but whether their residence was Stein or not is uncertain. There is no doubt that Stein was once a 'kongsgaard' or seat of a chieftain, and it is also a fact that a church of St. Olav was built in the small park, the ruins of which stand today. The church was in use regularly until 1581, and services were held on Midsummer Day until 1683 when it was destroyed by lightning. It was of Norman architecture and well built.

The owner at the time of the famous skirmish at Norderhov church (1716) was a 'storbonde' named 'Steins-Valdersen.' Colonel von Oetken led his Norwegian dragoons north from Lier across the ice to Stein, and then attacked the Swedish troop in Norderhov church and routed them. 'Steins-Valderstein' lived to the age of 101 and died 1741.

The existing house was built on old foundations in the 1830's, and possesses a ghost in the shape of a 'grey lady'—an old woman in a grey dress of another age. Stein is the largest estate in Buskerud, but everything ancient except the church ruins has vanished. The viewpoint of 'Kongen' lies on Stein property.

The slender spire of Norderhov church is visible for miles. Not far from Norderhov church lies *Tanberg* (Tornberg)—with grand views over Tyrifjord and Modum, towards Krokskogen's ridges on the one hand and Holleia with Telemark mountains on the other. At both Norderhov (Njardarhof) and Øvre Tanberg are echoes of the past—at the latter place a burial-ground with runes, arrowheads, spears, etc. One of the stones pictures Sigurd Favnesbane's fight with a dragon. In the garden at Tanberg was found in 1932 a wooden idol, supposedly on the site of a temple. Tanberg had its proudest days during saga times, when Alv of Tornberg married Ingebjørg, a sister of Duke Skule. The wedding took place at Bergenhus, and both Haakon IV and Skule were present; Alv was one of Skule's men and died in 1278. His son Erling went to Scotland with Haakon IV and was present at the death of his king. His son—Alv Erlingsson—was the most renowned of the 'Tornberg men' (see p. 90). The present family of Tandberg acquired Øvre Taberg in 1741, and one descendant who died in 1848 left 19 children and 101 grandchildren. The old man had welcomed Prince Oscar in 1833, when all the male members of his family fell in on one side of the entrance steps, and the females on the other. All were dressed in gaily coloured homespun, which the Crown Princess greatly admired. The estate has been assembled once again as it was in saga times.

Another old estate in Norderhov district is *Ask*, whose first known owner was a supporter of Harald Gille against Magnus III (1134). He was killed at the Battle of Fyrileiv soon after he had composed a poem (which has survived) in which he foretold he would never set eyes on Ask again. A barrow called 'Kongshaugen' lies close by, but after saga times Ask never played a noteworthy role as the residence of a thane. Near to Ask Peder Anker built the celebrated 'kjerraten' at Stubdal in Aasa—up which timber was hauled aloft 1,200 feet to Flaatevannet, whence it reached his smelting hut in Sørkedalen.

Ringerike's poet, *Jørgen Moe*, was brought up at the farm of Mo in Hole near Ask, and became a close friend of its owner, Gram; P. Chr. Asbjørnsen was sent up to Ringerike to school and shared with them the hunting and open-air life they delighted in. Hans Gude was often at Ask, and Welhaven, who roamed the hills with Gram. The latter, alas, pulled down the old house and erected the pretentious mansion of today in the style of 'Oscarshall.' He died in 1873 just as the house was completed.

Ringerike's nickel mine at Holleia was founded early nineteenth century, and by 1870 was producing one-seventh of the total world's supply. Discoveries elsewhere closed it down for awhile, but it reopened successfully during the first World War.

Some three miles north-east of Ask lies Ringerike's only town, *Hønefoss*, which received its charter in 1850. Its saw-mills had fabulous success at the time of London's Fire (1666): there were then no fewer than twenty-three saw-mills owned by citizens of Drammen. It lies on both banks of Aadalselva where it runs into Randselva—later to be known as *Storelva*. Hønefoss leapt to prosperity when the Bergen-Christiania railway was opened in 1909.

To the north of Hønefoss runs the valley of Aadalen, with its river Aadalselva draining the Lake of Sperillen. Mountains on its banks rise to 3,300 feet, and at the northern end of the lake the River Begna from Valdres flows in. A twin valley lying slightly to the west of Aadalen is Soknadal, in which at the station of Lunder the railway to Bergen pierces the western wall of the valley through the long *Haverstingstunnel*, from which it emerges in the centre of Lake *Krøderen* where it enters the Valley of *Hallingdal*. This great valley through which the Bergen railway was led in 1909, previously had most of its connexions with the outer world via Vestlandet; their souls were in the care of the Bishop of Stavanger until long after the Reformation. Their chief market for produce was at Laerdolsøra the week before midsummer, since transit of goods from Ustedal to Drammen took at least a week. If the ice on Lake Krøderen was not firm the return journey uphill took as much as three weeks with horses. Yngvar Nielsen made the upstream journey from Gulsvik to Nes in 1873, and described how the river boats were dragged round the waterfalls—including Sevrefossen—during several days. He tried to repeat his trip seven years later (1880) but could not find a man willing to undertake the journey, since the road had meanwhile supplanted river transport.

'Seters' are still in general use in upper Hallingdal, and most small farms have their own huts and grazing rights on two levels of height, the upper being used only in the warmest three weeks. Corn is still grown, but when, as frequently happens—it does not ripen, it is fed to cows as green food. At *Gol*, where Hallingdal takes a right-angled turn, an ancient road runs north-west to Filefjell through the lovely *Hemsedal*. Salt and corn used to be brought across the Vestland divide above Borgund and so down Hemsedal, but the railway has now put an end to such traffic and the roads exist for the tourists, being kept open only during the months of summer. The same applies to the road which runs south-west from Gol through Hol and Geiló to Haugastøl under Hallingskarvet, and then to Eidfjord in Hardangerfjord.

There is a magnificent stave church at *Torpo*, while the one that used to stand at Gol has been moved to Norik Folkemuseum in Oslo.

* * * * *

Between Lake Krøderen and *Numedal* lies an area of some thirty miles as the crow flies, and yet between them is room for the unique valley of *Eggedal-Sigdal* which runs into the mountain mass along the western slopes of *Norefjell*—a place now famous for ski enthusiasts. The upper part is Eggedal, the lower Sigdal, and together they are some forty miles in length. In its centre is the Lake Soneren, some 300 feet above sea-level, and they drain into Dramselva at Aamot (watersmeet). Wherever one wanders in this valley are memories of *Christian Skredsvig* who sketched it so diligently. He lived at the farm of Hagan, high up on the slopes above Eggedal church. The farms in all these high valleys are small; they were too remote to attract land-hoarders in times gone by.

* * * * *

From the junction of *Hokksund* on Dramselva the railway runs south-westward to the town of *Kongsberg*, which, like Kristiansand, came into existence at the behest of Christian IV—but for a different reason. In the summer of 1626 two goatherds found a glistening lump—whereupon the King decreed he was the owner of all *silver* in the len of Eiker, Sandsberg and Flesberg. On 16th March, 1626, 'thanksgiving services' were held in every church in Denmark and Norway. To begin with, methods of mining were primitive since explosives were not used until 1670, and annual yields were very variable. Charcoal, wood and timber were brought to Kongsberg under a system of compulsion, and in 1720 no fewer than 1,460 farms had liabilities to provide such necessities. Kongsberg was given a town charter in 1735, and made the 'capital' of all mining activities in Norway. For great hopes had been aroused in the eighteenth century, and by 1770 the town had a population of 10,000. Thirty years later there was acute want and poverty, and by 1814 there were no more than 4,000 inhabitants and it was actually proposed to abandon the town. Suddenly new hopes for silver were raised and so the town was saved, but nowadays there are no more than 220 men employed in the actual mine, out of a population of 8,000. The edict has now gone forth that the mines are to be closed down permanently in 1957, and so Kongsberg must live on secondary industries and its thriving tourist traffic. By 1937 the vertical depth of 'Kongens Mine' was 3,000 feet, though the average borings were no lower than 2,000 feet. The silver mines are now but a saga.

Kongsberg church is one of the largest in the country. Dating from 1761, it is the fortunate possessor of three beautiful chandeliers from Nøstetangen glassworks.

Attempts were made in early nineteenth century to establish ironworks in conjunction with those at Eidsfoss, to relieve distress among redundant silver miners. It was soon abandoned, and then the State established an arms factory, which is still working and is Kongsberg's main industrial activity. The 'Mint' is also situated here—close to the silver mines.

* * * * *

The valley of *Numedal* runs north from Kongsberg and is drained by the river Laagen, which eventually finds its outlet at Larvik in Vestfold. It has lived on its forests from times long gone by, and floatation to Larvik occupied many pairs of hands. Remote from central authority or the grasping grip of thanes and feudal lords, Numedal has retained its peasant character, and treasures many architectural gems of timbered architecture. Moreover, it is fortunate in the stave churches which have survived the destruction of the vandals who committed such crimes elsewhere a century ago. Those at *Rollag*, *Nore* and *Uvdal* are among the greatest treasures of Norwegian ecclesiastical buildings. 'Gamlekyrkja' in Uvdal from the thirteenth century is a masterpiece with its wealth of 'rosemaling' from seventeenth and eighteenth centuries.

Now power stations are swallowing the fosses, and the two at *Nore* (completed 1928) form the largest station under one roof in all Norway.

Uvdal is the district highest up Numedal, and thence the traffic across Hardangervidda used to be carried on down the centuries. Uvdøler were great pedlars, and carried their packs as far as Bergen across the mountains—Knut Hamsun has described their wanderings in his novel 'Landstrykere' (tramps). Seventy years ago Uvdøler were far more widely travelled than they are today, as they formerly spent much of their youth out of their home district. They were drovers of cattle across the wastes of the Hardangervidde, which they had bought in Nordfjord and other places in Vestlandet after disposing of their pedlars goods. Most of the livestock was sold at Kongsberg market, where buyers attended from many parts of Østlandet. This cattle-dealing only ended about a generation ago.

It seemed in the 1920's as though wild reindeer would be exterminated on the Hardangervidde north of Haukeliveien, but now numbers of tame reindeer have increased to *ca.* 6,000, and it may well be the census of wild ones would show a similar figure.

Emigration began from Numedal to America at a very early date. Three pedlars crossed the vidde to Stavanger on skis in 1837, and one returned to his native Vegglie in the following year with a story which his brother had written: 'Description of a Journey to America.' That same year he rejoined his brother across the Atlantic with a good following of Numedøler.

Now a fine mountain road runs from Uvdal to Geiló through distant Dagali. Most of the large lakes on Hardangervidde flow out through Laagen to Dagali, and so through Tunhovd into Numedal. Valley people used to fish those lakes, but now there is little reward. Tourists, however, carry on fishing in those lonely waters.

PART III

TELEMARK

CHAPTER X

PROVINCE OF TELEMARK

IN the very-long-ago the term *Telemark* was used for the up-country districts of the modern fylke of that name. The water-courses from that high-lying area united around *Norsjø* and flowed to the sea along *Skienselva*—all of that district became known as *Grenland.* The inhabitants of those two main districts were respectively referred to as 'teler' and 'grener,' the latter being mentioned by Jordanes (the historian of the Goths) as early as *ca.* A.D. 550. The 'teler' have shown themselves all through history to have been individualists who resented rule or discipline of any kind. They appear to have taken a prominent part in any and every anti-monarchical movement and to have defied governmental decrees from their remote valleys. The last notorious 'teler' rebel was none other than *Vidkun Quisling*, who was born in the lovely valley of Fryisdal. The 'grener' on the other hand have passed their lives down the centuries without being greatly affected by national disturbances, and hence it comes about that their districts are but seldom mentioned in Norwegian history.

The first person of note to have lived within this province was *Harald Grenske*—a great-grandson of Harald Fairhair—who was assuredly brought up somewhere in the neighbourhood of Skien. Harald Grenske married *Aasta* from Gudbrandsdal, and by her produced posthumously a boy Olav, later to become Olav II and to win a halo at the Battle of *Stiklestad* (1030). Harald felt, however, that he had made a poor marriage so when Olav was yet unborn he set out to Sweden to woo the formidable Queen Sigrid Storraade. The latter lady arranged a drinking feast, and when Harald, together with a Russian princeling who was also seeking the lady's hand, were completely inebriated, she had the house burnt over their heads and declared that thus would she treat any petty king who dared to win her favour. Aasta then married Sigurd-Syr of Ringerike, and there *Olav the Saint* was born and brought up along with their own son, later *Harald Haardraade*.

After Olav II acquired the sovereignty of Norway (1016) he experienced no difficulty in enforcing Christian practices upon Grenland, since missionaries from Germany sent by the sovereign lord of the area, King Harald Bluetooth of Denmark, had been working there for some sixty years before the coming of Olav. In Telemark, however, far away from the coast, heathen practices were so prevalent that they continued under more or less Christian veils until the beginning of the 19th century. At *Eidsborg* the ancient wooden figure of St. Nicholas used to be ceremoniously carried out of the church every Midsummer Eve and washed in the lake; this was to induce the saint to procure good harvests, just as the ancient Germans had done with the figure of Nerthus (*ca.* A.D. 100). This was the 'cult of fertility' in a Christian garb indeed! Olaf Isaachsen (1835–93)—often called 'the artist of Setesdal'—has thus described what he saw of 'Brokke-Fakse' at Rygnestad (in Setesdal): 'The upper section of a cylindrical ash-stub was filled with a figure of human shape about the size of a 12-year-old boy; the lower portion of the stub was adorned with twisted serpents such as are often portrayed in the older stave churches. The head of the human figure was covered with long curly hair and wore a beard; a crown or ring was set on the top of the head. The jaw was agape, eyes made of large bronze buckles, a belt round the waist, arms tucked in and hands folded closely together in front. Legs and feet were more or less forgotten.'

When Sigurd I returned from his crusade he introduced payment of *tithe*, and it is remarkable that thereafter Grenland was known as 'tiendelandet' (the tithe country) whilst Upper Telemark was called 'skattlandet' (the tax country). It seems obvious that the 'teler' refused to pay 'tithe' to priests when they had their own pagan idols, and so the King had to send tax-gatherers round to collect dues himself.

When the Civil War broke out (*ca.* 1130), Telemark showed

that it had preserved its purely peasant society, and there were no local 'thanes' to drag the people into strife since the masses took little or no interest in political action. Up in their remote valleys the peasants were telling and retelling the legends of their past, and when Saxo Grammaticus wrote his story of the great Battle of Braavalla and its hero Starkad, he used the version that was current in Telemark at his time (*ca.* 1180).

Waves of 'evangelism' were spreading across Europe in the first two decades of the twelfth century, and one result of these was the foundation of a nunnery, following the Rule of St. Benedict, at *Gimsøy*, Skien. This was sited on 'Klosterøya' between Klosterfoss and Damfoss, and had as its first abbess a sister of the great Gregorius Dagsson, Baugeid. Little or nothing is known of the history of this abbey, yet it acquired vast properties and did considerable trade on its own account.

Little is known of the activities of bishops before the arrival of Cardinal Nicholas Breakespeare at Trondheim (1152), but previous to that date the 'Viken kristenrett' (Christian law) (see 'East Norway') was not valid west of Brunlanes, i.e. it did not apply to Grenland. Cardinal Nicholas ordained that Grenland be embraced within the diocese of Oslo, whilst Telemark (except Kviteseid, Nisserdal, Fyresdal, Skagsaa and Mo) were placed under the Bishop of Hamar.

The leading figure in the party of Inge I during the Civil War was *Gregorius Dagsson* of Bratsberg, Skien—and with his death in Ranrike (Bohuslän), in 1161, the mantle fell on Erling Skakke of Sunnhordland, whose negotiations with Valdemar of Denmark are still the subject of speculation among historians. When the famous 'birchlegs' began their revolt under the leadership of *Eystein Møyla*, he received his main support from the peasants of Telemark, who rebelled owing to their extreme poverty and hatred of the landowning class.

It was probably in the time of Gregorius Dagsson that Grenland took over the administration of Telemark and both districts were merged into *Skiens-syssel*—at some later date this became *Bratsberg len* and, after 1660, *Bratsberg amt*. Since 1918 this area has been called the *Fylke of Telemark*, and the name *Grenland* from saga times has only recently been revived. There is an arm of the Skagerak called *Grenmar*, which as it narrows becomes Langesundsfjord; a right-wing newspaper in Porsgrunn has preserved the name Grenmar for the best part of a century. Bratsberg was the name of a mansion just north of Skien, which was originally the seat of Gregorius Dagsson. He, or his father, built the church on 'Kapitelsberget' whose ruins still stand. Ibsen wrote a verse about it.

The oldest industry in Telemark was the quarrying of whetstones. These stones were used as 'projectiles' at Fimreite (1184) and were frequently exported to England during the thirteenth and fourteenth centuries. Eidsborg was the centre of the work, which has been carried on until recent times. Peder Clausson wrote (*ca.* 1600) that the whetstones were floated down rivers and lakes.

Grenland had lain outside the scope of any of the law districts until 1224, when it was brought under Borgarting at Sarpsborg along with the rest of coastal Viken. This was an attempt by king and Church to create a stronger administration.

Henrik Ibsen and Skien

The greatest dramatist of the late nineteenth century was born in Skien on 20th March, 1828, in a house by the market-place which was destroyed in the great fire of 1886. When Henrik was only six years of age his father's unfortunate speculations landed the family in 'queer street,' and necessitated their removal in the following year to the small farm of *Venstøp*, which lies some 5 km. northwards of Skien's market-place.

The boy found much at Venstøp to fire his imagination, notably a copy of 'Harrison's History of London.' The illustrations in that volume stimulated his interest in drawing and painting, and from them he took his models for the puppet shows that so delighted his active childish mind. In later years he drew a vivid picture of his inconsequential old father in the character of Ekdal in 'The Wild Duck,' and employed the attics at Venstøp as the setting for many strange happenings in that great drama. The greatest ambition of his childhood was to be an artist, and two paintings of neighbouring mansions survive as evidence of that desire. Henrik Ibsen attended the primary school at the Fossum ironworks near by; later he trudged the three miles to Skien daily to attend a private secondary school until in December 1843 the entire family moved back to that town.

Ibsen was never happy at Skien; indeed his daughter-in-law wrote that the bankruptcy of his father, the idle gossip of the small town, the confined living quarters and much else besides, impelled him to break away from home ties and earn his own living. After he had settled down at Grimstad (see p. 151) early in 1844 at the age of fifteen, he returned to his native town but once (1850), in order to borrow money from relations for further education. The painful memories of his unhappy childhood are surely recorded in scenes he created in many of his plays—notably 'The League of Youth,' 'The Pillars of Society,' 'The Wild Duck,' and 'Peer Gynt.'

Skien has assembled personal relics of its great dramatist in a special 'Ibsen-section' at the Telemark Fylke Museum in Brekke gaard, on the heights high above the town where he first saw the light.

CHAPTER XI

INDUSTRIALIST LANDOWNERS

Ironmasters and Saw-mill Owners—and their Mansions

The earliest attempt to develop ore deposits in Telemark was made in the 1530's, when Christian III sent a Saxon expert to investigate possibilities. The peasants at *Seljord*, however, hindered his prospecting for copper there, and caused much trouble when ordered to provide the Germans with board and lodging. Armed forces were sent to subdue the 'telemarkinger' who had assembled in Annbjørndalen—a narrow valley in the upper part of Hjartdal. After they had been tricked into submission, five of them lost their heads.

The new openings proffered by the products of mines and forests during the seventeenth century, gave birth to an industrial aristocracy in Grenland. The new-rich families were mainly descendants of immigrants from Denmark and Germany, who had transferred to new-born Christiania and to Drammen from their native heaths in South Jutland which were in turmoil owing to the outbreak of the Thirty Years War. Skien and Porsgrunn housed them for a while, but once they had amassed some capital they built country houses in the neighbourhood of those towns, e.g. at Bolvik, Gimsøy, Mæla, Menstad, Borgestad, Fossum, Holden and Ulefos. Mansions tastefully furnished and decorated in the dignified style of the Georgian Era survive at the four last-mentioned places, where great traditions have been built up by such families as von Cappelen, Løvenskiold and Aall. Their frequent intermarriages make the story of their homes somewhat involved, for there are many features common to them all.

Borgestad

The oldest of those country seats is Borgestad, lying on the east bank of Skienselva between that town and Porsgrunn. A 'thane' must surely have lived here in the long-ago, since the foundations of a chapel from 1333 have recently been unearthed on the site. Borgestad was acquired by a citizen of Skien in 1648 —at the very time that increase in size of ships and their deeper draught necessitated the transfer of Customs control from Skien to Porsgrunn. The unique factor at Borgestad was the existence of a 'backwater' on the river bank, which enabled vessels to lie snugly out of the force of the current.

In 1702 Borgestad belonged to a General Arnold, who began building ships there, an industry which has continued to operate down to our own times. Arnold began his activities just as prices were soaring: that he was responsible for at least a portion of the present building is shown by the date 1698 on a cellar beam. It is also known that he was honoured in that house by a visit from King Frederik IV in 1704.

The first *Løvenskiold* to live at Borgestad acquired it in 1731. He was of the third generation in Norway to bear the surname of *Leopoldus*—before his father was ennobled as *Løvenskiold*. Father and son bought up large areas of forest, and all the ironworks in Telemark, during the slump which followed the close of the Great Northern War. When better times came along in the 1740's they were the 'kings' of industry and commerce in the Province, which was at that time known as *Bratsberg Amt*. The wife of that first Borgestad Løvenskiold was daughter of the renowned Bishop Deichman of Oslo, and after that powerful prelate died—it was said of a broken heart at his treatment by the King *—her mother settled down at Borgestad, where her room survives and is still known as 'bispinnens kammer.'

Bartholomeus Herman Løvenskiold (1729–88), who succeeded to Borgestad and Bolvik, wrote a 'Beskrivelse over Bratsberg Amt'—a gold-mine of eighteenth-century local history. His daughter married *Jacob Aall* (1750–1826), a son of a wealthy Porsgrunn merchant whose grandfather had migrated from the village of Aal near Ribe (Jutland). After Jacob had spent a couple of years in England, he sold his parents' house at Porsgrunn to *Severin Løvenskiold*. That house is today known as 'Kammer-

* See 'East Norway and its Frontier.'

herregaarden' after that famous Severin—of whom more later.

Jacob Aall bought Borgestad from his father-in-law, Bartholomeus Løvenskiold. When his first wife died he married a wealthy lady, and Borgestad became for a long time a centre of hospitality of great repute. Jacob's own appetite was so prodigious that he is credited with consuming an entire goose to fortify himself before entering his carriage at 4.30 a.m. to drive to Christiania. When the post-Napoleonic slump arrived, Jacob was one of the first to fall, and was compelled to sell Borgestad—though he and his wife continued to live there until their ends came.

In 1823 Borgestad was acquired by *Realf von Cappelen* (1791–1853), whose first Norwegian ancestor had come to Norway from Bremen together with the famous ironmaster Krefting, of Bærums Verk (*ca.* 1640); Realf had himself been brought up in Denmark. His grand-daughter, Anna Sofie von Cappelen, brought Borgestad to *Gunnar Knudsen* (1848–1928) when she married that famous future statesman in 1880.

Gunnar Knudsen had studied shipbuilding in England before taking over Borgestad (1881) from his father-in-law. He later founded the 'Borgestad Shipping Company' (1904), and will ever be remembered in national history as its Prime Minister during two critical periods—1908–10 and 1913–20. A radical, although a traditionalist and somewhat of an autocrat, he instituted a scheme of State Insurance, and so laid the foundation of the 'welfare state.' Probably no party politician in Norway has ever exercised such a decisive influence on the legislation of his day. He died in 1928, when his three sons took over his Grenland activities.

The greater part of the mansion, as it stands today, dates from the time of General Arnold (*ca.* 1700); the similarity in design to its thirty-year-older neighbour at Larvik—across the border of Vestfold—is obvious.

Fossum

Some three miles north of Skien at the junction of two rivers lies *Fossum*, the chief seat of the *Løvenskiold* family who have lived here for nearly two and a half centuries.

8. Knut Hamsun at his farm Nörholmen

View from Krokskogen over Ringinke (' Kongens Utsikt ')

9. Merchant's mansion, now Town Hall, at Arendal

Venstöp, Henrik Ibsen's childhood home

The Saxon prospector sent by Christian III found quantities of iron ore. According to reports, the first hammer at Fossum was set up in the spring of 1539, and was operated on royal account for some years with but meagre results. Christian IV was the first to enthuse over the potentialities of Norwegian iron production, and as the demand for guns, shot and armour was immense in the early days of the Thirty Years War, he brought all the small ironworks in Norway under his 'Iron Company.' Smelting began at Fossum in 1625, but production was very limited, and from the Crown Fossum passed to private interests.

Work began again energetically in 1668, when the works were extended and large numbers of excellent cannon were produced. They were transported to Skien on specially designed carts, often drawn by no fewer than eighteen horses. This activity continued at fever heat until the close of the Great Northern War (1720) and then died away.

The works were taken over by Herman Leopoldus in 1739—the very year that he was ennobled under the title *Løvenskiold*. They passed to his son Herman (1739–99), who was obliged to divorce his flighty wife, Ingeborg Akeleye, when she ran away with the notorious Christian Conrad Danneskiold-Laurvigen (see p. 63). Fossum later came to his brother Severin (1743–1818) who had married Benedicta Aall (aunt of both Niels Aall of Ulefos and Jacob Aall of Nes).

Their son *Severin* (1777–1856)—later to become the most famous of all the Løvenskiolds—took over Fossum in 1803. As amtmann for *Bratsberg* from 1803 he was the leading figure in that Province for several critical years. It so happened that he was at Kiel in 1807, when the news arrived that the British had seized the Danish Fleet in Copenhagen. Severin made the strongest representations to Crown Prince Frederik that it was essential for Norway's continued existence he should immediately reverse the policy he was pursuing towards England. At Eidsvoll, Severin worked with Count Wedel and Jacob Aall in the minority party that favoured Union with Sweden; he always referred to those days as the 'unhappiest six weeks of my life.' Appointed 'statsminster' in Stockholm (1828) he soon got into trouble with the masses in Norway who looked upon him as a reactionary—'an aristocrat who upheld the conservative notion of constitutional monarchy.' When Karl Johan dissolved the Storting in 1836 Severin Løvenskiold assumed full responsibility for the King's action, since he regarded 'sovereignty by the People as dangerous and revolutionary—freedom of the Press as incompatible with a good order of Society.' He dubbed the Storting: 'this queer association of arrogant self-rulers': yet the credit for the Resolution on 'the freedom of the flag' in 1838 was exclusively his. During the Crimean War he found himself in violent opposition to King Oscar I, since the 'stattholder' favoured a Russophile policy.

Fossum comes to life in a description of the reception there in 1849 of Oscar I with Queen Josephine, Prince Gustav and Princess Eugenie. The royal party was driven from Skien in fourteen closed carriages with a mounted escort of farmers. A torchlight parade of Skien's citizens took place in the evening in front of the mansion, while bonfires blazed all around and guns boomed. The aged 'stattholder' presided over the celebrations with immense dignity—'a remarkably imposing old man, both mentally and physically, and with a will of iron.'

In 1854 the 'stattholder' sold the properties to two of his sons, but during the 1850's production of iron declined and smelting ceased altogether in 1867, chiefly owing to competition from cheap English coke iron. The saw-mills were transferred to Bøle (4 km. south of Skien) where woodpulp mills were erected in 1887 drawing power from waterfalls. When transmission of electric power over long distances became practicable, a larger woodpulp mill was built near Skien in 1908.

The mansion of *Fossum* stands as the old 'stattholder' left it—exactly as it looked on its completion in 1818. The Løvenskiold name and tradition continue to keep alive at Fossum the atmosphere of byegone days.

Holden (*Ulefos Jernværk*)

Ironworks were started at *Holden* in 1657 by Preben von Ahnen—that 'junker' who achieved so much in the Fylke of Nordland.

Shortly afterwards they came into the hands of the fabulously wealthy Dane, *Anders Madsen*—a citizen of Tønsberg who also owned Eidsfos and Ulefos for a time.

In 1676 an energetic owner, *Halvor Borse*, put new life into the undertaking. In order to avoid the excessive cost of transport of ore from Arendal, he bought up fresh deposits in Vollsfjord, which became known as *Bolvik*. Borse was murdered in 1702: the perpetrator of the crime was never brought to book. His son Joachim (1679–1739), and his two sons-in-law got themselves involved in some shady transactions—one of the latter was put in prison where he lost his reason whilst proclaiming his innocence.

The only one of the three brothers-in-law to clear himself was Herman Leopoldus (1677–1751), who was later ennobled as *Løvenskiold*. He purchased Holden with Ulefos Jernværk, which in his days were the largest ironworks in Norway with the solitary exception of Fritzøe (Larvik). Herman Løvenskiold succeeded in weathering the slump which followed upon the Great Northern War, and passed Holden with Ulefos Jernværk on to his son Severin (1719–76): who, however, moved to Denmark where he founded the barony of *Løvenborg*, and built one of the four sections of that most attractive royal *Palace of Amalienborg* in Copenhagen. The youngest of his two grandsons took over the two Grenland properties, and moved up from Denmark to reside in the manager's house—the first of its owners ever to live on the property. He later returned to Denmark, and then the Løvenskiold Saga at Holden with Ulefos Jernværk died after a full century.

Holden was bought in 1835 by *Diderik von Cappelen*, whose father Diderik (1761–1828) had been Skien's representative at Eidsvoll (1814). In 1822 Amtmann Baron Wedel-Jarlsberg put forward Diderik's name as deserving of royal recognition in a citation, which eulogized his energy and self-sacrifice in forwarding the common weal during the disastrous conditions pertaining at the close of the Napoleonic Wars.

His son, Diderik, born 1795, was the first Cappelen at Holden. He had been educated in Denmark and England before he married a Løvenskiold, who gave him two sons and many daughters. The younger boy—*August*—gained great fame as an artist: his favourite subjects were landscapes among the vast forests of Holla and Landsmarka. In his letters, which have been published, he gives vivid descriptions of life in those unfrequented wastes, relating how on one occasion a bear came trundling by as he sat at his easel. The letters make it obvious that life at Holden was very pleasant a century ago.

Diderik Cappelen retired to Copenhagen in 1854, and passed over his Grenland holdings to his elder son *Severin Diderik*, who then built the present mansion around the kernel of the old manager's house.

As a result of the industrial activities the population had increased considerably, and Severin Diderik wanted to present his parish with a commodious new church in gratitude to the peasants who had worked so hard to minimize destruction to the countryside during the recent inundations. The church was built but, alas, at the cost of the little old church which had stood there since the twelfth century. He utilized its stones for his new barns and outbuildings. Such vandalism was all too common practice in that graceless age: his daughter-in-law has made such amends for his 'crime' as lay in her power by ensuring preservation of what remained of the ruins. Severin Diderik was an able and energetic man, who modernized his works and bought up large areas of forest.

The mansion at *Holden* retains many treasures, including a large collection of the paintings of August Cappelen, valuable furniture, and antiques inherited from ancestors and relations at Holden, Mæla, Eidsfos, Fosseholm, Austad, Hafslund and Vækerø. The family of *Cappelen* which has owned it for more than a century and its forests for twice that period, has created a living tradition. They have combined the noble traditions of the past with progressive measures necessitated by the requirements of today.

The name of 'Holden, Ulefos Jernværk' is treasured in the world of Art, and not alone for the elegant designs on stoves produced there continuously throughout the last three centuries.

Ulefos

One last estate in Grenland remains to be described, namely *Ulefos*, around whose name that of *Niels Aall* will ever revolve. In the seventeenth century it lay too remote to tempt any magnate to erect a dwelling, and when it came to the Arnold family, they continued to reside at Borgestad. Jacob Aall—the first of that name out of Denmark—went to London (*ca.* 1680) at the time that city was being rebuilt after its Great Fire (1666), largely with timber from East Norway. His son *Niels* (the first) was sent to Porsgrunn under the care of an Englishman established in business there—who was himself brother-in-law to Herman Leopoldus. Young Niels Aall was made attorney to the recently ennobled *Løvenskiold* who had bought Ulefos. Niels, who continued to administer that estate even after he had set up in business on his own account in 1734, was thrice married to girls in Porsgrunn 'society.' Niels built three houses in that town, amongst them that later known as 'Kammerherregaarden,' which still stands. He withdrew from all activities at the age of seventy-six, and then his elder son Jacob settled down at Borgestad, whilst the second *Nicolai Benjamin* remained at Porsgrunn.

Nicolai Benjamin Aall (1739–98) had been tutor in the family of the renowned Bishop Gunnerus of Trondheim—he having been destined for the Church. The death of his elder brother forced him to enter business, but he retained all through life the humanistic outlook of his early days. He was a close friend of Bernt Anker. Before 1782 he became owner of *Ulefos*, ran his own ships to England whither he dispatched as many as ninety cargoes annually. His son Jacob Aall of Nes (Aust-Agder) has left us detailed accounts of life in Porsgrunn during the latter half of the eighteenth century. Nicolai Benjamin left four sons, of whom Niels (the second) took over his chief property of Ulefos—Jørgen remained at Porsgrunn and Jacob bought Nes. Those three brothers all became national figures who played vital roles in Norwegian History.

Niels Aall (the second) had received his grounding at schools in England and France before he set up in business on his own account with the Ulefos saw-mills and vast forests in Telemark. He launched forth in the first of the seven 'fat' years of neutrality, when it was said that anyone could make a fortune who had the slightest desire to do so. Optimism reigned in Norway as never before, and we have the account books which Niels kept so meticulously at Ulefos to tell the tale of astronomical profits. Then in 1807 began the seven 'lean' years, with the bankruptcy of Aall's chief connexion in Copenhagen following upon the outbreak of war with England. Aall was in a critical position, but matters improved when two years of trading by 'licence' began (1810–12), and enabled him to pull through temporarily. Not until after the war ended (1815) did difficulties arise which proved to be insurmountable.

During the 'golden years' Niels Aall had indulged in a considerable building programme, of which some fine homes survive today. In 1810 he enlarged and adorned *Brekke* gaard in Skien, which is now the fylke museum. His chief work was, however, *Ulefos:* originally built as a summer residence, it appears to have been translated *en bloc* from Southern Europe—though its architect was Rawert from Copenhagen. Niels stated that he had been influenced in choice of design by the English country mansions he had seen when young. Ulefos occupies a commanding position on a height close to the outlet of Eidselva into Norsjø. Among the wall paintings are some painted by the Swedish Count Mörner while he was a prisoner here after capture at the skirmish at Toverud (1808). Many purchases of English furniture were made by Niels' London agent, and a splendid library also remains which has been assembled during many generations. Ulefos is far more than a rich man's home—it stands as a monument of a dignified age which has elsewhere faded away with all its grace and beauty.

Standing lower than the mansion, Niels built (1814) an agent's house called 'lille Ulefos'—to the designs of the same architect as that of its contemporary, Fossum.

When Christian Frederik was elected King of Norway (1814), Niels Aall was given the delicate task as leader of a deputation to England to work for consideration of Norway's plight. It was a sad journey, since the three members were met with an eviction order as they set foot ashore, and so returned without any achievement whatsoever.

Shortly afterwards he was given another difficult task, when together with Collett he had to treat with the Swedes for a truce, and signed '*The Convention of Moss*' (August 1814) much against his will. He employed every persuasion to induce Christian Frederik to fight: 'in order to disillusion those holding power of the abominable belief that human beings can be used as objects of trade—to be brought like cattle to market.' When Christian Frederik left the country, three men carried out the functions of a State Council during the interregnum, namely Rosenkrantz, Niels Aall and Jonas Collett. Niels was the only one who refused to join a government after Union with Sweden; he withdrew from politics and confined himself to his business interests.

Yet before long he was driven to humiliate himself by accepting a loan from Karl Johan, which permitted him to carry on for a while until he had to take the bitter decision to sell up—a fate he shared with so many other great Norwegians in that doleful era. Jacob Aall at Borgestad and Jørgen Aall at Porsgrunn were ruined in the early 1820's, and in 1830 Niels had to sell Brekke gaard to ease his position. Within a couple of years there was yet another ruinous slump, and Niels had to face his creditors who, fortunately, were mostly his own relatives. He sold out entirely in 1839, when his son Hans bought Ulefos.

Niels Aall recorded his reminiscences, which make it clear that he was a steadfast and fervid patriot. Soon after the attack on Copenhagen by the British (1807) he wrote to Consul-General Wolff in London concerning 'this abominable act of treachery.' He states his belief that the English People disapprove of the action of their Government, but 'I am only surprised that such a contemptible body of men are tolerated as leaders by a humane and honourable People.' After he and his wife had celebrated their golden wedding, he died at Ulefos on 23rd October, 1854. A leading modern historian has called him 'a worthy branch of a noble trunk—he was indeed a great man.'

Ulefos is one of the most splendid mansions in all Norway. Few possess such ancient family traditions which are so jealously guarded as here. Care was taken by Cato Aall that the house may be preserved for all time with its beautiful face and figure, and —mercifully—Aalls are living there today. They have their family mausoleum at Romnes church, a twelfth century structure.

CHAPTER XII

BYWAYS OF HISTORY IN TELEMARK FYLKE

A Perambulation of Grenland

THE westernmost valley of Grenland is Drangedal, whose river drains Tokevatn and flows into the Skagerak at *Kragerø*. The fylke has a very short coastline whose westernmost outpost is at Ellingsvik, some 4 miles from the ancient harbour of *Portør*,* which is itself at the western entrance to the harbour of Kragerø. 'Norway's riviera' is the name now applied to the coast around Kragerø—an ancient small town where time has stood still, and which consequently has attracted many of Norway's best artists—Fritz Thaulow, Jean Heiberg and Per Deberitz. In 1666 Frederik III granted Kragerø 'town rights' and decreed that 'its inhabitants may reside unmolested there, and not be compelled to remove to Skien.' A famous son was the painter Theodor Kittelsen. It existed for long on its timber export from the well-forested upland of Drangedal; now it lives on fish and summer tourists.

At the outlet of the much-frequented Skienselva lies *Langesund* which has for centuries been the outer harbour for the series of inland waterways in Western Grenland. 'Portus de Langesunde' is mentioned as an export place as early as 1398 in English records. In 1576 Peder Clausson Friis wrote: 'The most remarkable and renowned ladested in Norway is Langesund, where every year several hundred ships load timber for masts, spars and deals which are floated down from Skien and from far in the interior, and sold in this harbour.' The open sea is just round the point, but the harbour is a snug one between mainland and Langøya. Boat-building has been an occupation for centuries:

* For Portφr see 'Sφrlandet.'

Tordenskiold's famous galley ' Løvendals gallei' was constructed here. It has two dignified patrician's houses—Wrightgaarden and Raadhuset.

Further up Langesund and on either side of the fjord stand the twin towns of *Stathelle* and *Brevik*—the former is still a ladested whereas the latter was granted its town charter in 1845. Brevik, which is the last coastal town that has a 'Sörland' atmosphere, has lived on its shipping since its inception: it was the birthplace of *Cort Adeler*, the famous admiral who gained fame in Dutch service in the seventeenth century.

Where Porsgrunnelva swells out into Frierfjord stands the modern industrial centre of *Herøya*, where the factories of Norsk Hydro produce untold quantities of fertilizers which are exported to all the countries in the wide world. The workmen live in ancient *Porsgrunn* at the mouth of the River Skien—with the town of which name it is likely soon to be joined since population grows apace.

At *Porsgrunn* is the finest porcelain factory in Norway which was founded by a brother-in-law of Gunnar Knudsen, who for a time was himself its manager. Export of timber was its livelihood in days gone by, its harbour took vessels of deeper draught than Skien's, but its near-by neighbour Herøya now eclipses the old town which is largely a dormitory for Norsk Hydro's factory.

Skien is the capital of Telemark. Henrik Ibsen was born at Skien and there is a street and park named after him—as also a statue. Ibsen's childhood memories were not happy ones; his father moved there after financial ruin in 1835. The old town is mentioned first in 1184, and was granted full town privileges by Haakon VI in 1358. A strange industry was the shaping of whetstones, production of which continued as late as 1949—in the Middle Ages it might have been looked upon as an 'armoury' of stone projectiles. The mansion of *Brekke*, built (1810) by Niels Aall of Ulefos who laid out its pleasant park, is now the fylke-museum.

An industry that flourished till close of nineteenth century was the cutting and export of *ice*. It was sawn at Ulefos, and the old dam at Bolvik which had been used for the ironworks was employed after 1860 as an 'ice-dam,' with a runway down to the icehouses on the fjord. All the waterways of Upper Telemark (except Fyrisvatn, Nisservatn and Tokevatn) drained through Norsjø into Skienselva, and 'natural ice' was easy to transport.

The canal system is little more than fifty years old, yet it is already hallowed as an ancient traffic route. The two main watersheds of Upper Telemark are an *eastern* one through Møsvatn, Tinnsjø and Heddalsvatn, and a *western* one through Totak, Bandak to Ulefos. Both have their sources far beyond the fylke boundary to the west, and the whole Telemark system of waterways is most involved. Along the eastern system of waterways the twentieth century has taken charge in the age of electricity. Two towns house the factory employees of *Notodden* and *Rjukan*, which have no links of any kind with life as lived of old. Into the north end of Tinnsjø four valleys run down—Tassungdalen, Maardalen, Gøystdalen, and Vestfjorddalen. Sixteen kilometres up the last of them stands *Rjukan*, by the harnessed waterfall of the same name, in a deeply-scored valley where the sun seldom penetrates during the summer months and for five winter months is never seen at all. So Norsk Hydro has constructed a rope-railway to take its workpeople occasionally up on to the vidde to glimpse the orb of the sun.

Water-power has brought 'big industry' to Vestfjorddalen, *Vemork* (1910) being one of the largest power-stations in Norway. Together with its two other stations it constitutes the largest concentration of harnessed power, and from the factories is exported 'salpeter' to the wide world.

The lower courses of the waterways rise very gradually; indeed at Norsjø, which is 180 km. from Skien, the height above mean sea level is only 50 feet. This section of locks was completed in 1861, and once in Norsjø the lake provided access to Ulefos. At that spot is the terminal station of the Bandak-Norsjø Canal which was built 1887–92, and which links innermost Grenland with the sea: there are fifteen locks between the two terminals, and the rise is 170 feet. The steamers here run all the year round—assisted by a small icebreaker. From the west end of Bandak

Lake the dales rise steeply—the stream from Totak and Vinje comes down from the north in a deep ravine.

In *Vinje* communication has been maintained with Vestlandet owing to the seasonal migration of numbers of goatherds seeking summer pastures in Telemark. *Aasmund Olavsson Vinje* the poet was born in a shack in Vinje which is now a place of pilgrimage under the name of 'Plassen'—whence he had magnificent views over fjell and vidde. In our own day we have perhaps the leading living Norwegian poet *Tarjei Vesaas* of Telemark, and folk-song in this district is richer than at any other spot in Norway.

One of the most beautiful parts of Telemark is *Rauland*—all around Totak. Here stand precious remnants of ancient timber buildings, and at *Vaa*, beyond Møsvatn, lived 'Dyre Vaa—the boldest peasant in Vinje parish,' and today the famous sculptor of the same name. At the west end of the lake is Øygaarden, where *Myllarguten* (1801–72), the renowned fiddler spent his last years in extreme poverty, but gained immortality when a statue was erected of him with his fiddle at the station of Nordagutu. His real name was Tarjei Augundssøn, called 'master of masters' and he possessed an immense repertoire.

The people of Upper Telemark always had a reputation for individualism and resistance to authority. Halvard Graatopp's revolt in 1438 brought swift retribution, and Peder Clausson Friis described them (*ca.* 1580) as: 'shameless bodies of the Devil whose chief delight is to kill bishops, priests, bailiffs and superiors—and who possess a large share of all original sin.' The The early Socialist movement of Marcus Thrane (*ca.* 1850) was well spread throughout Grenland whilst Solum and Bø declared majorities for a republic in 1905. In Grenland's industrial population there is a large percentage whose views are extremely to the left.

Gustav Adolph *Lammers* was priest at Skien when he began his break-away movement from the Established Church (*ca.* 1860); Ibsen used him as a model in 'Brand.'

The wild districts of Upper Telemark would have been largely impenetrable had it not been for the employment of *skis;* winter was ever a better travelling period than summer. Ski-running, originally a necessary means of communication, was brought to Oslo from Telemark as a sport in the nineteenth century and from there the fashion spread to the Continent, indeed the world.

The mountain of *Gausta* is Norway's Fujiyama, and there it lay isolated after the Black Death had depopulated the districts round Møsvatn.

Notodden is the youngest town in Grenland, not having obtained a town charter until 1913; now it is but a link in the chain of Norsk Hydro's installations between Rjukan and Herøya. Saw-mills were opened at Tinnfoss as far back as 1873, but 'salpeter' transformed it into a town, and it had a 'golden age' during the First World War. It suffered in the depression that followed the end of that upheaval, for all its operations were transferred to Herøya at the place of shipment. Somewhat later Norsk Hydro found other industries to keep Notodden thriving.

Away in the east of Grenland lies the valley of *Siljan*, the old name for which was Slemdal. Bishop Claus Pavels visited it in 1793 and recommended it to anybody who wished to end his days in philosophic peace. As recently as the 1920's someone wrote of *Kilebygda* (just west of Skien). 'It is, thank God, still not discovered by tourist agencies and recorded in their routes.' All that is past—and cars rattle everywhere. The valley of Siljan drains into the sea to Farris in Vestfold, and most of its forests belong to Treschow-Fritzøe at Larvik. Løvenskiold of Fossum owns several thousands acres on the east side of Norsjø right up to the Buskerud boundary; on its west side, around Ulefos, vast areas are owned by the Cappelen and Aall families.

Of ancient churches that of *Seljord* is of stone from mid-twelfth century, but the greatest glory in the fylke is *Heddal* stave-church: 'The richest and most beautiful of all that type of church in Norway.' It was here that Tidemand painted his most famous picture 'A Catechization.' It dates from *ca.* 1250 and was dedicated to the Virgin Mary.

PART IV

SØRLANDET

10. Glass goblet from Nöstetangen with English Royal Arms

Below : Interior of Holt Church from 1757

11. Head of Vigeland's statue of Henrik Wergeland in

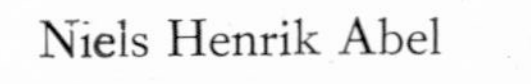

Niels Henrik Abel

CHAPTER XIII

AGDESIDEN

An Ancient Kingdom in Sørlandet

SØRLANDET (the south country) is a name of recent invention, used to denote the territory anciently occupied by that branch of the mighty tribe of 'ryger' which Jordanes (*ca.* A.D. 550) referred to as *Egder*. Long stretches of its coastline—known as Agdesiden—are fringed by off-lying islands which have provided a sheltered channel for vessels all down the centuries. Its upland dales have ever been heavily forested, and habitation only possible in a series of confined valleys. These are completely cut off from one another by mountain ridges, and scarcely a vestige of a track has existed to permit overland communication until the dawn of this century.

Sørlandet, which is made up of the coastline and its immediate hinterland in the two fylker of *Aust-Agder* and *Vest-Agder*, was so christened by its very own poet, *Vilhelm Krag*, who died in 1933. Not only do its inhabitants speak a unique dialect, but their characteristics and way of life differ in many essential respects from those to be found elsewhere in Norway. Why should this be so?

A modern historian has advanced a very convincing theory that a Swedish conqueror and his armed following infiltrated into the lands of the 'Ryger' and 'Egder' about A.D. 800, and set up a *Kingdom of Sørlandet*. This eventually stretched from a point some ten miles east of modern Arendal as far as Tungenes, near Stavanger. Among the characteristics peculiar to this area are:

(1) That 'borgs' (earthworks) from the Migration Period (A.D. 400–600) are numerous within the supposed limits of the kingdom, whilst no traces of such defences have been found east of Arendal.

(2) That within the frontiers of this supposed kingdom, land was valued for taxation under *utskyld* (a Swedish term)—the unit of assessment was 1 *hud* (hide), which was divided into 12 *engelsk* (english). These terms were in use within the limits of the old kingdom down to the nineteenth century, and were never employed elsewhere in Norway. (It is fascinating to speculate whence came the term 'engelsk'. The finds at Sutton Hoo in Suffolk (1939) evidence contact with Uppsala—might it not be that the Anglians of Suffolk joined forces with the Swedes in the building up of the 'Utskyld' kingdom of Sørlandet?)

(3) It is possible that it is the language of the 'svensk-engelsk' conquerors which survives in the *sørlandsk* dialect of today. It is noteworthy that the dialect spoken in Holt—the next parish eastward of Tromøy—is *not* sørlandsk but østlandsk. At Boknfjord—the northern frontier of the supposed kingdom—the dialect changes to vestlandsk in Ryfylke.

(4) Whenever Snorre mentioned Rogaland he refers only to its northern portion, i.e. Ryfylke, north of Boknfjord.

(5) It is possible that the original inhabitants of Agdesiden (the 'egder') were driven up the valleys into the 'corner' of Raabyggelaget (*raa* means 'corner')—an ancient administrative district which embraced remote *Setesdal*, and may account for the strange dialect and customs current in that distant valley which bear little relation to those in use in the remainder of Norway today.

A wealth of fable and legend is woven around Sørlandet and its ancient kingdom, perhaps the best known story being that of *Starkad and Vikar*. According to Gautreks Saga, a King Harald of Agder gave Tromøy (off Arendal) to Storvirk, whose son Starkad—a Nordic Hercules—was deluged with presents including a massive gold ring, by Harald's son Vikar. Starkad returned the compliment by presenting Tromøy to King Vikar—a tradition survived on Iceland that a 'kongsgaard' stood on Tromøy, owned by the Agder kings Harald and Vikar.

King Harald (Rufus) of Agder had a lovely daughter, *Aasa*, who was desired by Gudrød Veidekonge, the mighty king of Vestfold. The latter sailed to Agder with a fleet—either to

Tromøy or to Huseby in Lista—whence he abducted the girl, after killing King Harald and his son. In due season Aasa gave birth to Halvdan Svarte (809–834), and before the little fellow was a year old she avenged her father and brother by procuring the murder of her husband. Then Aasa hurriedly returned to her old home in Agder to bring up her son, who took over his Kingdom of Agder at the age of nineteen (828–853). He then extended his dominions to include most of Østlandet, married the Lady Ragnhild (daughter of the King of Sogn), and with her produced *Harald Fairhair*. *Aasa of Agder* was buried by her son in the Oseberg ship (850–875).

Another fascinating legend from Agder during those early days concerns *Ragnar Lodbrok*, who is credited with marrying a young girl from Kraaka in Spangereid, supposed to be the daughter of Sigurd Fafnesbane and Brynhild. The virgin put up a surprising defence of her chastity, and yielded only after having compelled Ragnar to take her 'for better for worse.' They then produced several children, of whom *Sigurd Orm i Øie* (born *ca.* A.D. 790) inherited all Viken and Agder as far as Lindesnes. Little more is known of this King Sigurd, who had a cast in his eye which appeared as though a worm had curled itself round the pupil.

The Conquests of Harald Fairhair

The unification of Norway was brought about by Harald Fairhair at the epoch-making Battle of *Hafrsfjord* (about 890). It was a victory over the rulers of 'The Kingdom of Sørlandet,' and was fought on their northern frontier—just off their most northerly defence position on the island of *Utstein*. Harald occupied Utstein, the key to the south-west kingdom, and the saga writer sings a pæon of praise at the overwhelming victory. Harald's chief opponent at Hafrsfjord was 'Kjotve the Wealthy of Kvina,' a native of whose valley of Kvinesdal was the famous skald *Tjodolv of Kvina*, who is believed to be the earliest of Norwegian historians. That poet lived for long at the 'kongsgaard' of a nephew of Halvdan Svarte—King Ragnvald of Vestfold—where he composed *Ynglingotal*. Thus it happens that posterity owes an immense debt to the poet from Kvinesdal in Vest-Agder who has preserved the story of the royal family of Ynglingene.

Tjodolv of Kvina was later attached to Harald Fairhair, and was present at many events which led to the unification of the realm. When that king discarded the sons born to him by Snefrid—the bewitching Lapp girl from Tofte in the Dovrefjell, who had administered an aphrodisiac whereby Harald fell from grace—one of those unfortunates found refuge with Tjodolv at his 'hall' in Kvinesdal, until he met death by drowning off Jæren.

Shortly after Hafrsfjord, Harald Fairhair was much at his 'kongsgaard' at Tromøy (Arendal) where, according to Egil's Saga, he had installed one of his relatives, Tororm, as bailiff. Tororm of Tromøy was collecting taxes in Telemark from a thane named Aasgrim who lived at Tinn. When Aasgrim—who was obviously a typical individualistic and rebellious 'telemarking'—refused to pay, one of Tororm's slaves cut off Aasgrim's head. The latter's son, realizing his danger, then embarked at Langesund with all his belongings, to settle down in Iceland—but en route just popped in at Tromøy and burnt the 'hall' of Tororm over his head and those of his retainers.

It would seem that Harald Fairhair appointed one 'Audun' as his 'earl' in Agder, and in Grette's Saga (composed *ca.* 1300) is a tall story of Audun's attempted murder by a gang of malcontents, led by one Torstein. The latter fled to Iceland on the advice of a thane in Siredalen, and Harald then sent a punitive expedition to remove their heads. The quarry escaped, however, and King Harald's men spent that winter in Iceland in 'Kvinverjadal' (the valley of the people of Kvinesdalen). Torstein was an ancestor of Sæmund Frode.

After the Battle of Hafrsfjord, Agder lost a large proportion of its thanes, who migrated to Iceland with their families and retainers rather than submit to the sovereignty of Harald Fairhair. The most celebrated of these was Øksna-Tore of Vest-Agder, whose descendants founded some of Iceland's most distinguished families—one of whom was none other than *Erik the Red*, the colonizer of Greenland.

Even before this mass migration to Iceland, the Orkneys and

Shetlands had attracted some of the best sons of Agder and Rogaland. Place-names in both groups of islands made it appear that they were colonized almost exclusively by folk speaking the dialects of the 'egder' and 'ryger.'

Christianity comes to Agdesiden

After the victory of Haakon (I) the Good at Reheia near Avaldsnes (935) over Erik Blood-axe, the last heathen king of Norway, the latter fled to Aust-Agder and thence to Jutland. Ten years afterwards his brother Gudrød—one of the 'sons of Gunhild'—landed on *Lundgardssida* to secure the person of a man named Sote, who had gone there to claim his inheritance which had been appropriated by a friend of the evil Queen Gunhild; Sote was hanged on the spot. Lundgardssida, which lay between Askerøy in Dypvaag and Portør in Skaatøy, is perpetuated in the name of *Lyngør*.

Christianity was forced upon Agder by Olav (I) Tryggvesson, who met with little opposition in that thinly populated district, abandoned as it had been by its families of thanes who had mostly fled to Iceland and the Scottish isles. Olav Tryggvesson sailed away from Oslofjord to his defeat and death at Svolder (1000), and in his company in that decisive action was mentioned Torgeir Tjodolvsson of Kvina—surely a relative of the great skald?

After Svolder, Norway was partitioned among the victors in that battle in such a manner that Erik Jarl of Trøndelag was granted the west coast as far south as Lindesnes and the Danish King, Svein Forkbeard, the coastal districts in south Norway to the eastward of that point. Erik Jarl's control of Vest-Agder would have been nominal in view of the pre-eminence of Erling Skjalgsson of Sola in that area, whilst the Danish sovereignty was exercised through petty kings.

After Olav II (the Saint) had won his great victory over Svein, the brother of Erik Jarl, at Nesjar in 1016, he summoned the peasants of Agder to their 'tings,' where all acclaimed him 'king.' A leading thane here in his reign was Gudleik Gerdske—so nicknamed because he traded with Gardarike (Russia)—whilst yet another renowned viking was Eyvind Urarhorn of

Aust-Agder. He plundered far and wide in the lands across the North Sea, in Frisia and the Baltic, and gave Olav II invaluable help at Nesjar with his well-armed vessel of twenty thwarts. His later exploits on behalf of King Olav in Ranrike (1017) were of great value to his king.

After twelve years as Norway's king the position of Olav (the Saint) became exceedingly dangerous with the arrival of Canute the Great in Agder (1028). The latter summoned the peasants to their 'tings,' where they acclaimed him 'king' and gave hostages for their good behaviour. A relic of those far-off days was a runestone at Fennefoss in Evje, inscribed: 'Arnstein erected this stone in memory of his son Bjor, who died in Godwine's army when Canute went to England.' Godwine was presumably an Englishman who led a division in Canute's army (1029); the stone is now in the University collection.

In 1028 Olav (the saint) left Tønsberg to face up to Canute, but was only able to recruit a meagre force among the outer islands on Agdesiden. He lay for a long time during early winter at *Seløyerne*, just north-west of Lindesnes: when he proceeded north he joined battle with Erling Skjalgsson and killed him at Utstein (see p. 214). That was the last occasion the 'Saint of Norway' appeared in southern Norway.

Little is known about Agdesiden during the reigns of Magnus (I) the Good, and Harald Haardraade, but a highly coloured story is told by the saga-writer about old Torkel Dyrdil, an uncle of Olav Tryggvesson. He had been appointed sysselmann of Agder by that King, and must have been a very old man when Magnus the Good suspected him of secreting royal funds collected during the rule of the English Queen Alfifa and her son Svein (1030–35). The old man had hidden the royal monies in the entrails of a stuffed goat, and when Magnus at Torkel's express desire cut off the head of the animal a shower of coins rolled out (*ca.* 1040). In Magnus the Good's saga it is written that when Sigvat Skald returned from Rome he heard—when lying in Hillarsund near Mandal—that Olav had been killed at Stiklestad, and there and then composed a verse based on the flight of ravens he had just seen passing over Hillarsund.

Magnus the Good lay among the Seløyer in 1047 with his fleet, when on his way to Denmark and death. At Seløy he was visited by Torfinn Jarl of the Orkneys who had murdered some of his guardsmen: there was no reconciliation and Torfinn thought it wise to put to sea quickly and return to the Orkneys.

Saint Magnus and Ragnvald Jarl

Kale Sæbjørnsson was a leading thane in Agder and a fine skald besides. He lived near Arendal where his equally gifted son Kol came of age *ca.* 1095, and father and son accompanied Magnus (II) Barefoot on the second of his Scottish campaigns. Old Kale was mortally wounded in the famous Battle of Menai Straits, Anglesey and, to compensate Kol for the loss of his father, King Magnus presented him with a bride in the person of Gunhild, a daughter of Earl Erlend of the Orkneys and a sister of Magnus (later the Saint). King Magnus handed over several properties on the islands as a wedding gift.

Kol's brother-in-law Earl Magnus (the Saint) was murdered in 1115 at the instigation of his relative Earl Haakon, but Kol made no immediate attempt to take Vengeance on the mighty Haakon. He remained quietly at his home in Agder awaiting a favourable opportunity. Meanwhile his son *Kale* grew up to every form of youthful excellence: a poet who played the harp and could read runes, fairhaired and in physique a Hercules.

When towards the close of the 1120's Earl Haakon of the Orkneys died, his son Paal became 'earl' and declared his independence of King Sigurd I of Norway. Thereupon at the wish of his mother, Kale changed his name to *Ragnvald*, in memory of the gifted Earl of that name who had been a friend of Olav the Saint and was killed by Torfinn the Mighty. In his early years he went on several trading voyages, during one of which, when only sixteen years old, he made friends with the future King Harald Gille in Grimsby. At an audience of Sigurd I in Tønsberg that king transferred the half-portion of the Orkneys which had belonged to Magnus (the Saint) to Ragnvald, but he was unable to enforce his rights there as Earl Paal was in sole possession and refused to surrender any part of the islands.

Bishop William of the Orkneys was induced to travel to Agder and was there persuaded to obtain canonization of the murdered Earl Magnus: his enshrinement took place in Christ church, Birgsaa, on St. Lucia Day (13th December), 1135. By this time Harald Gille was King of Norway, and he immediately confirmed Ragnvald's earldom which his predecessor Magnus the Blind had retracted. In 1136 Ragnvald seized the Orkneys from his Shetland base, and ruled as sole 'earl' for the King of Norway until he went on crusade (1152). After his return thence he had to wage a bitter struggle for three years (1155–58) to retain supremacy over the Orkneys.

It is a great thought for Orcadians that two famous sons of Agder—Kol and his son Kale, *alias* Ragnvald Jarl—obtained the canonization of their St. Magnus, and laid the foundations of his glorious Norman cathedral immediately to the south of the then town of Kirkwall. Although it was later extended considerably, much of the original structure stands today just as erected by Ragnvald, before he met a violent death in Caithness in 1164.

The Great Civil War on Agdesiden

There were few families of the status of 'thane' in Sørlandet, and therefore little partisanship existed there during the struggles of the disastrous Civil War. *Sigurd Slembe* indulged in much piracy from the ancient port of Portør, which lay near Kragerø and within modern Telemark fylke. On one occasion in the summer of 1138 in company with the blind King Magnus, he made a surprise landing at Lista and killed the agent of King Inge I, before he and his blind king fled to Haalogaland. (See 'North Norway.)

On one occasion the 'bagler' king *Erling Steinvegg* led his fleet as far west as Hesnesøyerne, in Fjære, with the intention of proceeding further north. Having received intelligence that the 'birchleg' bailiff of Vest-Agder had mobilized forces in Kvinesdal and lay at Hitterøya, Erling made haste to overtake them. The birchlegs finding escape impossible, took refuge ashore and left their vessels to the mercy of Erling, who sailed into Egersund unmolested.

King Inge II and Haakon Galen left Viken with a large fleet in the autumn of 1207 with the intention of driving the 'bagler' out of Bergen. Little Haakon IV was on board with Haakon Galen, and all the fleet lay at Seløyerne many weeks where they suffered cruelly from intense cold. Haakon IV was to return in 1224 to inflict defeat on bands of 'ribbunger' who were ravaging all over Agder, especially around Mandal. Following the complete dissolution of the 'ribbunger' pack, Haakon IV met Duke Skule at Seløyerne, and with a fleet of large ships sailed away to Denmark.

Once again (1256) Haakon IV came to Agder from Bergen to meet a priest named Elis, who had just returned from Spain in company with a Spanish Embassy, whose leader was a priest Ferdinand. They brought important dispatches from King Alfonso. The King met them at *Randøsund* and learnt of the proposal that his daughter Christina should marry one of the brothers of Alfonso X (the Wise).

Agdesiden during Hansa Monopoly

During the fourteenth and fifteenth centuries the German Hansa held Norwegian commerce in a firm grip. Their merchants had little use for Sørlandet since timber was its sole product and all the cities of the Hansa—except Hamburg—drew their supplies of forest products from the Baltic coasts near by. An eminent living Norwegian historian has stated that 'throughout the Middle Ages Agder was off the map,' and it is a fact that little is known about Sørlandet until the Reformation, when the development of the use of water-power for saw-mills coincided with heavy demands for deals in the outer world.

The Frisians, however, had at all times brought a variety of commodities to Norway, and returned with cargoes of timber, dried fish, furs, etc. Two of their favourite ports of call on Agdesiden were Lyngør and Tromøy, and a small island in Tromøy sound is still called Frisøy. There was also at all times a useful trade with Jutland, especially during the thirteenth century when Norwegian shipping was in a flourishing condition. Even as late as the fifteenth century when the Hansa monopoly was at its height there were yet a number of ships sailing out of the fjords and creeks along Agdesiden.

The Dutch required oak for shipbuilding, and at one time oak forests thrived abundantly along the south coast. These were, however, so denuded by mid-sixteenth century that King Frederik II prohibited all export of oak. After water-powered saw-mills were introduced (*ca.* 1530) oak was replaced by fir, for deals and—most important of all—masts, as the main export commodity.

* * * * *

After the Crown of Norway began to be worn by members of the Royal House of Denmark, they granted fiefs (len) to the nobles of that country in the absence of any Norwegian nobility. In Agder the greatest of these was *Hartvig Krummedike* who was first granted Lista len. In 1443 his popularity there was such that the peasantry petitioned that he might come back to them since he had given efficient protection from the Dutch pirates who had ravaged Norway's coasts in 1440, under the plea of rendering help to King Erik of Pommern. Krummedike twice married rich Norwegian heiresses and thereby acquired vast properties—in Aust-Agder alone he owned in 1456 no fewer than fifteen large estates.

For administrative purposes in very early times the whole of 'Egdafylki' sent representatives to Gulating—at Gulen at the entrance to Sognefjord, and during the reign of Olav II (*ca.* 1020) 29 representatives had to attend from Agder. Under the 'Universal Law' of Magnus V (1274) numbers were reduced, but it was laid down that Agder should send 12 representatives, Otradal 4 to Gulen, and Setesdal 2. The two latter districts were embraced in an administrative unit called *Raabyggelaget*—a term which meant dwellers in remote districts—and this decree of Magnus V is the first occasion that Setesdal occurs in history. It would appear that there were three names for sections of Otradal, viz.: Setesdal in Valle, Otradal the mid-section of the valley, and Tovdal through which ran Tovdalselv.

Towards the close of the Middle Ages Egdafylki was made up of a number of syssler: Lista, Mandal, Aust-Agder (or Nedenes) and Raabyggelaget. There were times when each of these four districts had their own 'lensherre' or royal bailiff, but most usually Nedenes (in Øiestad) took the lead, and at *Nedenes kongsgaard* dwelt the overlord of Agdesiden until Christian IV ordered Palle Rosenkrantz to remove to the newly built 'kongsgaard' near his pet town of Kristiansand (1641).

Christian II Returns to Norway (1531)

The change-over from the Roman Catholic Confession to the Lutheran appears to have been made on Agdesiden without a blow being struck, or even a murmur of disapproval since priests and public continued the old rites for several decades. The great event during that religious upheaval was the arrival of the exiled King Christian II at Hesnes in Fjære with such remnants of his fleet as had survived the gales it had run into since leaving Holland. The armada that was to reconquer Norway for the Roman Faith sailed from Medemblik on the Zuider-Zee on 26th October, 1531, carrying about seven thousand men. The following morning a violent storm arose which lasted several days and scattered the fleet. Some ships were driven to the Scottish coast, others off Jutland, whilst not a few were shipwrecked off Rogaland.

Christian II himself arrived at Hesnes with only four ships, and from that harbour issued a proclamation on 5th November to his 'beloved, good and faithful subjects in Norway of all estates. . . .' Owing to bad weather he had to remain at Hesnes until the 7th November, and landed some twelve hundred men in Oslo on the 9th and 10th without opposition from its citizens.

The total failure of this expedition, and the ensuing imprisonment of Christian II for eighteen years, is a story outside that of Agdesiden.

* * * * *

Christian II's adherents in Norway were now doomed men, and the ruthless Tord Rød—Christian III's commandant at Bergenhus—surprised several of them off Lista and decapitated every man. Then came upon the scene a native of Agdesiden as bailiff—*Stig Bagge*—who was granted the 'len' from 1536–42.

He was an energetic man whom Peder Clausson says indulged in executions of refractory peasants to an alarming degree. After the revolt in Telemark caused by the King sending German mining prospectors had been quelled, troubles broke out in Raabyggelaget which spread to Nedenes, where they found the bailiff in bed at the kongsgaard and stabbed him eighteen times. Then they took the long journey to the 'hall' in Lista where Stig Bagge was wont to dwell, but found him absent. Stig quickly collected men and stifled the revolt at birth. Stig Bagge's own end was quartering and to be laid on wheels after the Dutch had caught him off their coasts in 1542. An aura of romance survives around the name of that brutal adventurer.

Piracy was a terror to the coastal folk all through the sixteenth century, and especially during the wars between England and Scotland. The English were most feared, and in a report from Flekkerøy to Christian III (1558) it was stated that English and other pirates landed and robbed their cattle and provisions. Also Frenchmen—usually called 'Dunkirkers' were a plague to the inhabitants. Things had got so bad by 1550 that a fort was built on Flekkerøy to provide a base for Norwegian warships which, however, were unable to mitigate the evil to any great extent. The coastal flotilla thus formed did, however, do splendid work in the seven years war with Sweden that ensued.

* * * * *

A curse to the people of 'Nedenes len' at the close of the sixteenth century was its lensherre *Erik Munk*, a favourite of Frederik II who amassed vast properties hereabouts. Historians have compared him to a Turkish Pasha who respected neither the rights of the Crown nor the individual. He lived at the Manor of Barbu (now Arendal) and allowed the 'kongsgaard' at Nedenes to decay. The peasants on more than one occasion collected funds to send a deputation to the King at Copenhagen to petition for Erik Munk's removal, but he invariably succeeded in surprising the conspirators and taking vengeance. At long last he had to face a commission appointed to enquire into his misdeeds, and having been forcibly removed from Barbu by a Royal warship, he was imprisoned in Earl Bothwell's old place of detention at Dragsholm in Denmark, where he finally committed suicide in 1594 and was buried under the gallows outside that castle. His son was the famous polar explorer Jens Munk, who was born at Barbu Manor.

Erik Munk was, however, responsible for an active commercial policy which had lasting effect on the prosperity of Agdesiden. In his greed for wealth he established several saw-mills, and sold deals in large quantities to Danes and Dutchmen who brought their vessels to the river mouths. In one year no fewer than 150 foreign ships loaded timber in the len of Nedenes—a trade which resulted in the creation of such future towns as Arendal, Grimstad, Lillesand and Risør. Moreover, Erik Munk built the first iron-smelting hut in Nedenes len at Barbu (1574).

* * * * *

The life of *Peder Clausson Friis* (1545–1614)—the most remarkable Norwegian scholar of his century—was spent almost entirely in Vest-Agder as priest at Sör-Audnedal, and archdeacon of Lista. He is best known as a translator of Snorre, but was also a linguist, historian, topographer and natural scientist. At the request of Statthin Axel Gyldenstjerne he began to translate Snorre's royal sagas in 1599, which came into the hands of the famous Ole Worm who caused them to be printed in 1633. Norwegians revere his memory mostly for his 'Norrigis Beskrivelse'—an account of the internal situation in Norway soon after the new order under Danish suzerainty and the Lutheran Confession had been established. As far as Sørlandet is concerned he lived in Vest-Agder, visited Aust-Agder in 1592 and neighbouring Grenland in 1576.

* * * * *

A famous harbour on Agdesiden was *Merdø*—the forerunner of modern Arendal. It is first mentioned in 1524 when a Danzig ship seized a Scotsman 'at Mardø in Norway.' In the archives of Norway's last Archbishop, Olav Engelbrektsson (which were recovered from Germany three centuries after the death of that prelate), a letter was found dated Leith, 7th June, 1528. It was from one John Straughton of Edinburgh to acknowledge receipt from John Creighton—servant to the Archbishop—of a gun which had been taken from a Stralsund ship 'in the harbour of Merdoe in Noroway.'

During both the sixteenth and seventeenth centuries Danish, Dutch, German and Scottish ships frequented Merdø, but Norwegian vessels only seldom. Peder Clausson (1592) mentioned 'the celebrated harbour of Mardø' and also 'the renowned ladested Arndal.' In 1646 Christian IV ordered Hannibal Sehested to furnish him with a sketch of Merdø and its surroundings, whilst as late as 1780 'The English Pilot' called the approaches to Arendal 'The Harbour of Mærdow.'

Hamburg was a frequent destination for timber cargoes, with which city Erik II had concluded a special treaty in 1296. Hamburg had no desire to be dependent on the Wendish ports of the Hansa for its timber supplies, and even as late as 1641 Christian IV inserted a clause in Kristiansand's 'town charter' granting freedom to trade with Hamburg.

When the so-styled 'omlandsfarten' (traffic with neighbouring countries, i.e. between the North Sea and Baltic via Skagerak and Kattegat) began, Agdesiden became of interest to foreign shipping as providing harbours of refuge and source of supplies of fresh water and food. This transit traffic was non-existent during the Middle Ages when the Hansa tolerated no competitors and the narrow waters were their 'Tom Tiddler's ground.'

* * * * *

King Christian IV was faced with three major tasks:

(*a*) To defend Norway against an agressive Sweden.

(*b*) To increase revenue by advancing the interests of the bourgeoisie at the cost of those of the nobility.

(*c*) To strengthen Denmark-Norway's defence against the Germans during the Thirty Years War.

In order to realize the above objectives it was necessary to establish towns at important strategical points, and preferably where at the same time sufficient trade could be attracted to make them self-supporting.

The old king decreed the foundation of the City of Kristiansand on the southern fringe of the country, which he believed satisfied the above conditions.

CHAPTER XIV

AUST-AGDER FYLKE

THE old name for the eastern part of Agdesiden was *Nedenes* 'Len'—later 'Amt'—at which spot a 'kongsgaard' stood whence the 'lensherre' administered most of Agdesiden (and at times the whole of it) until King Christian IV moved Palle Rosenkrantz (1641) to *Oddernes* (*Kristiansand*).

Travelling eastwards along the coast one enters 'Agdesiden'—as also *Aust-Agder* Fylke—at Gjernestangen. The old name for this spot was *Rygjarbit*, the eastern limit of settlement of the tribe of 'ryger' in the very-long-ago.

The easternmost small port in the fylke is *Risør*, where only a few fishermen had their huts when Dutch vessels began to call there for timber (*ca.* 1570). As early as 1607, however, two inns had been opened to serve Dutch sailors—yet Peder Clausson had made no mention of Risør. The 'Lord of Nedenes,' Christoffer Gjøe, owned it in 1640: he fitted mooring rings in the rocks, built beacons and laid out buoys. A timber church was built in 1647, which survives: in those days Jutes sailed across the Skagerak in search of timber.

The traders at Risør were compelled to maintain residences in royal *Kristiansand* after its foundation in 1641, and to answer their names at a roll-call of its citizens on Midsummer Day. Although granted a 'town charter' in 1723, the good folk of Risør were forced to make annual payments to Kristiansand for yet another century.

When *Mary Wollstonecraft* paid a visit to Risør in 1795, she found its people in good heart and conducting a considerable timber trade as well as building their own ships. She had a feeling of being in a prison, hemmed in by steep hillsides: she failed to imagine how its inhabitants could absorb any form of culture. Their lives were spent peddling goods, drinking and smoking—

the men were seldom without a pipe in their mouths from dawn to bedtime—and they never dreamt of opening windows. They had plenty of money—more than they knew what to do with—and their women were laden with trash 'like sailors girls in Hull or Portsmouth.' Yet, strange to say, they were beginning to read translations of good German literature.

At Risør, as at many other loading-places along Agdesiden, young seamen brought back Dutch wives after serving in ships of that nation. Hence it comes about that even to this day such Dutch Christian names as Jan, Cornelius and Reimert are not uncommon in Sørlandet.

The harbour of *Lyngør* lies near *Dypvaag* and protected by the islands of Ytre Lyngør. When some British men-of-war chased the frigate 'Najaden' into Lyngør harbour (1812), that last major unit of the Dano-Norwegian Navy perished, and most of her dead were buried in a common grave on Askerøy, some 500 yards west south-west of Lyngør. A marble slab was inserted in a low wall by the grave: 'Passers-by! Step with reverence, for here rest 75 brave naval ratings, among whom lieutenants G. Grodtschilling and P. Buhl. Faithful to God and King they all fell during the night between 6th and 7th July, 1812, fighting on board the frigate 'Najaden' against the superior might of Britain.' Both lieutenants had brilliant records in numerous previous engagements with British brigs. Norwegians regard the youthful Captain Stewart, who was only twenty-four at the time of the action, as 'a little Tordenskiold' since he ran untold risks in manœuvring his unwieldy line-of-battle ship 'Dictator' in such a confined channel.

On 18th August, 1847, the Norwegian Government erected the present monument in the form of a broken mast. The centenary was celebrated in the presence of King Haakon VII, when Norwegian and Danish guns fired over the battlefield in honour of the long-dead heroes.

The port of *Tvedestrand*, at the head of Oksefjord, first came into use as the place of shipment for the products of *Nes Verk*, which were iron and timber. Lying in the parish of *Holt*, Nes Verk is now one of the largest and most beautiful surviving mansions in Sørlandet. The founder of its fortunes was *Ulrich Schnell*, a descendant of a Haderslev merchant who had migrated to new-born Christiania (*ca.* 1630). At Nes, Schnell concentrated various iron-workings in the neighbourhood (1738) and set up several saw-mills in the surrounding district. He obtained special licence to export timber from Tvedestrand, where he built warehouses and dwellings for his employees. In later life he handed over control to his son, Jacob, and moved to Porsgrunn.

Then in 1799 came *Jacob Aall*, who was to become such an outstanding and honoured figure in the national history of Norway. Born at Porsgrunn (1773), he was a younger brother of the famous Niels Aall (1769–1854) of Ulefos in Telemark. Jacob was a model employer at a period when the economic life of Norway was flourishing under neutrality: he modestly wrote that 'such conditions minimized the probable results of my own lack of experience'—for his real interests lay in academic pursuits. By 1811 he had made a fortune, whilst at the same time modernizing his plants and making astounding improvements in agricultural practices throughout the district. In his smithies he produced anchors, cables and saw-blades, and also owned three privileged saw-mills, corn-mills, many ships, and was a large exporter of timber. When, following 1814, Norway lost her tariff preferences with Denmark, Aall worked up a market in northern Germany—a proof of the high quality of his products. The stoves cast at Nes during his time are museum pieces today. Remarkable are those cast in the shape of draped figures in the classical style.

Jacob Aall was a friend of Denmark where he had studied in youth, and was at all times anxious not to break with her. He declined for long to follow the lead of Wedel to link up with Sweden, until at length 'the good of the fatherland made it necessary that I should do so,' and economic chaos and events on the Continent caused him to change allegiance at Eidsvoll. His fine library at Nes survives to keep green the memory of one of Norway's finest men in her hour of crisis.

The main building at Nes was erected by the elder Schnell (*ca.* 1740), but it is the halo of Jacob Aall which outshines all other memories. His direct descendant controls the steel factory which began producing steel in 1859; the last stove was cast in 1870. 'Nes Steel' is of highest quality for tools: it is familiarly known as 'Aallestaal,' after its originators.

The church at *Holt* possibly dates from twelfth century and has a very ancient font. Much of the beautiful interior decoration is the work of Torsten Hoff, who adorned Vor Frelsers church at Oslo.

Arendal

The port of *Arendal* was but an insignificant 'ladested' previous to the foundation of Kristiansand (1641), though a growing population was settling down at the mouth of the River Nid, and on the small islands of Tromøy, Merdø and Hisøy. The iron-works at Barbu and at Neskilen lay close by, whilst up the river were a series of saw-mills. Barbu ironworks had been founded in 1574 by Erik Munk (see p. 140), but eventually under its monopoly the 'Iron Company' acquired Barbu, which was closed down in 1659.

It was, however, the gold workings around Arendal which aroused Christian IV's highest hopes, and drew him to the spot during his last visit to Norway. From the meagre output he caused the famous 'brilleducater' to be coined (1647): Christian refused to credit the reports of his assayers that the quartz was not worth while reducing so, as was to be expected, his most important mine, known as 'Christian Qvart Guldgrube,' had to close down in 1651.

After Kristiansand had been granted its 1662 privileges, the people of Arendal were described as 'citizens in Kristiansand.' Relations between Arendal and Kristiansand continued to worsen despite every effort of the Viceroy, Ulrik Frederik Gyldenløve, who championed the old King's pet town. Financially, Arendal was sweeping ahead, one reason being that its possibilities at the mouth of River Nid gave it a far richer hinterland than that of the 'royal' town. More than one 'Stiftamtmann' wrote after 1660 that Kristiansand's upland was the most wretched for anybody to try to scratch a living from. It is therefore not surprising that Arendal's merchants refused to move to Kristiansand as ordered by royal decree.

The journal of the Norwegian travels of King Christian V records that he spent one night at Arendal (1685): also that it and Risør were frequented by Dutch and English vessels in search of timber. When some twenty years later his son *Frederik IV* arrived (1704), the diary kept by his half-brother, Ulrik Christian Gyldenløve, describes the journey from Risør to Arendal thus: 'When we got clear of that slippery place we came into open sea, and then went ashore at a house where we dumped our drunken coxswain and took another aboard.' At Arendal the King was rowed in his barge under an arch of honour covered in greenery, which was suspended between two ships. No fewer than sixty vessels were at anchor, all full-dressed with bunting: 'It was a pretty sight, but did not enthuse me since I had been sitting in the rain for more than ten hours and had not closed my eyes the whole night through. . . .' Next day the King visited Merdø, and returned to Arendal for dinner. In his sermon the priest 'went to great trouble to explain in detail how the rite of circumcision was performed by the Jews.'

The last three decades of the seventeenth century had been most favourable for Norwegian shipping. The English Navigation Acts of the 1650's had put an end to the transport of timber to that country in Dutch bottoms, which gave a tremendous fillip to the Norwegian ship-building industry and to its overseas shipping. Arendal took full advantage of these circumstances which were all the more valuable after the Great Fire of London (1666) created such a demand for Norwegian timber. The wars of Louis XIV at the close of the century gave neutral shipping a great opportunity and trade a considerable impulse, the more so since Denmark-Norway came to an agreement (1691) with Britain that their trade with France should not suffer interruption.

The presence of large numbers of foreign sailors in the little port led to frequent breaches of the peace. One serious instance occurred in 1700 when a student from Riga started a row which was taken up by the nine hundred foreigners then in port; the disturbances lasted several days.

The Treaty with Holland (1701) menaced Norwegian shipping and, moreover, put an end to the 'defensive ships,' i.e. auxiliary warships sailing as merchantmen under national subsidy. Depression ruled until the close of the Great Northern War (1721), and then conditions improved once again. At the outbreak of hostilities with Sweden (1709) the government had been at its wits' end to organize defence, so when the good folk of Arendal voluntarily offered to build and man three galleys—the *quid pro quo* being freedom from paying rates to Kristiansand—their proposal was accepted and their patriotism remembered. Thus it came about that three years after the Peace, Arendal was granted a preliminary 'town charter' (7th May, 1723); henceforth there were two towns on Agdesiden. Ditlev Wibe—that most efficient 'stattholder'—strongly advised this step, and made it clear to the Government that Arendal had brilliant prospects, whereas those of Kristiansand were very limited. In actual fact the timber trade of Arendal had never been transferred to Kristiansand despite the latter's 'charter of privileges.'

Thereafter Kristiansand's privileges covered only that stretch of coast which is now that of Vest-Agder; Arendal acquired the coastline of the modern province of Aust-Agder. The business of separation was effected far from peacefully, but both towns had by then acquired their own traditions, so that local patriotism did not permit disputes to be protracted. As late as 1670 Kristiansand had owned hardly any ships: its citizens were merely agents for Dutch shippers. It possessed far less capital wealth than Arendal, where lived families who had accumulated considerable riches and among whom were many enterprising shipowners at the moment (1725) when Denmark imposed a monopoly of corn importation into southern Norway in favour of Danish corn. Arendal vessels sailed to the Baltic and Jutland to load grain, and by 1765 its fleet had so multiplied that it had become the principal shipping town in all Norway.

After that year freights fell alarmingly, but Arendal owners held on to their ships and thus had a flying start when trade revived again. During the 'golden years' of the French and American wars (1776–1806) Arendal shipping earned fabulous sums, and when 'Dunkirk' privateers began bringing their English prizes into the port the shipowners bought them up at knock-out prices. The unfortunate English crews frequently implored protection from their French captors. Most Arendal merchants had their own agents in London and Amsterdam, yet skippers brought back payments in hard cash, and foreign coins were always in plentiful supply.

Kalm (the Finnish botanist) wrote (1747): 'Most of the town is built on piles over the water,' and until the disastrous fire of 1863 Arendal lived up to its nickname 'Little Venice.' After that conflagration the complex of narrow canals intersecting the town—which had enabled ships to load and discharge in its very heart—were filled in. Thereby Arendal lost much of its picturesqueness, but mercifully the fine house—the second largest timber building in all Norway—built by Morten Kallevig in 1810 still stands, and is now the 'City Hall.' Nothing can, however, ever spoil its natural setting, and Arendal will therefore always remain a picturesque gem.

Opposite to the town on the island of *Tromøy* stands a venerable church, in part of dressed stone from *ca.* 1075, though considerable additions were made in the eighteenth century. Sailors have always valued it as a landmark, which is made more distinctive by reason of the ancient fir-tree standing alongside.

On the lower reaches of the River Nid, and within the district of *Oiestad*, was formerly a considerable estate and large mansion called *Nedenes kongsgaard*, where lived the royal bailiff until his translation to Kristiansand (*ca.* 1640). Here was born Niels Rosenkrantz (1757–1824) who, when Foreign Minister, urged King Frederik VI (1810) to break with Napoleon and join up with Britain. His younger brother, Marcus of Borregaard—who was born at Vigvold in Randøsund—played a prominent role during Norway's struggle for independence. The destruction of *Øiestad Church* (*ca.* 1075) by fire in 1900 was perhaps the most grievous cultural loss ever sustained in Aust-Agder.

A charming legend surrounds a gravestone formerly imbedded in the wall of *Fjære* Church (built before 1200), the most precious old building in the fylke. A female figure wears a crown on her head, and the inscription beneath states that she was '. . . Isaak's daughter, of the glorious family of Norwegian Kings and Danish princes.' The Danish leopard and Norwegian lion make it probable that she was a daughter of Isaak Gautsson (*ca.* 1281)—possibly Cecilia, or another child of whom nothing is known. This was the stone which caused an early nineteenth century archæologist to assert that it covered a daughter produced through illicit intercourse between Audun Hugleiksson and the Princesse de Joigny (who might have been the betrothed of Haakon V, *ca.* 1295); that, however, is nought but a fable. The inlet where the lady's ship was wrecked is still called 'Princesse-vika'—near Hesnes.

Grimstad lies within the ancient parish of Fjære. At Hesnes close by Christian II found anchorage for the insignificant remnants of his Armada (1531). Although Peder Clausson does not mention Grimstad, there was nevertheless an inn here as early as 1607 for the benefit of visiting sailors: fifty years later it became a 'ladested.' Kalm wrote (1747) that he visited it and none but sailors lived there: he also noted it was a favourite haunt of smugglers. When the *Froland* ironworks were founded it became the port of shipment of their products.

In 1811 an English brig was blockading the coast to prevent corn supplies reaching Norway. Its boats entered the harbour on one occasion but were so roughly handled that they suffered numerous casualties.

Grimstad, which is one of the prettiest little ports hereabouts, houses an *Ibsen* museum that recalls his early days when apprenticed to a local chemist. In that house he wrote satires on the citizens, sonnets to the many girls he courted, and his first drama, 'Catalina.'

Some 15 km. above Arendal, ironworks were established under the name of *Frolands Værk*. These later came into the possession of one of the most remarkable men of his age, Johan Frederik *Classen*, who obtained concessions to export and import through Grimstad and thus to by-pass Arendal and its customs dues. On the death of 'General' Classen the King granted a favourable loan to Frolands Værk, and fixed contracts to deliver cannon-balls to the Government. These were passed on to the Dey of Algiers, and to the Sultans of Tunis and Tripoli as tribute to obtain freedom of passage for Dano-Norwegian ships along their coasts.

As from 1786 *Hans Smith* was sole owner: he built a new mansion, and continued the manufacture of cannon-balls, though many beautiful designs of stoves were designed by *Ole Nielsen Weierholt* (1718–92). That artist was a native of the province, having been born at Austre-Moland, and is without question the leading exponent of rococo in these parts. His work remains in many churches on wood and iron adornments.

Bankruptcy led to a forced sale of Froland in 1832, and soon after it came into the hands of a Copenhagen firm of bankers—for whom ironworks at such a distance were not an attractive proposition. So *Treschow* acquired them (1845) and operated Froland in conjunction with Fritzøe. Then came intense competition with England and America and the works closed down (1867), when saw-mills replaced their former activities.

The ruins of the abandoned ironworks are still visible, and in front of the big house is a monument to the world-famous mathematician *Niels Henrik Abel.* Born near Stavanger (1802), he spent his unhappy boyhood in the rectory at Gjerstad (near Risør) and died at Froland Værk in April 1829. He came to spend Christmas with his fiancée, Christine Kemp, who was governess to the Smith family, when tubercular hæmorrhage set in, followed by pneumonia. Although entirely without private funds and little appreciated during life, he nevertheless revolutionized the science of mathematics in spite of his short span of life. The room in which he died has been retained exactly as it was during his fatal illness, and there he penned the last treatise to be created in his astounding brain, a synopsis of his thesis on 'addition' theory, for the thesis itself has disappeared. His grave is in Froland churchyard—near the old timber church from 1716.

In the neighbouring parish of *Landvik* was a noble seat, which was granted to a *Friis* by Frederik II (*ca.* 1580). Not a few residents here today claim descent from Friis ancestors: several farms have been in the possession of their families for more than three centuries. In Eide parish stood an ancient seat, *Nørholm*, which was in ruins when the world-famous novelist *Knut Hamsun* acquired and restored it in 1918.

Lillesand is built on the ancient 'odel' estate of *Lofthus*, and Christian—the rebel of that name (*ca.* 1780)—was seized here at a house which is still standing. *Tingsager* gaard belonged to the Rosenkrantz family, but no nobility ever lived there. A few gracious houses from *ca.* 1800 remain at Lillesand to mirror the style of an age of good taste. The port lies in the parish of *Vestre Moland*, where a fine old house from 1780 stands. It is called 'Mads Møglestue's House' and was inherited by his daughter *Emerentze Stenersen*, a remarkable personality who farmed and owned ships on a large scale. Vestre Moland Church was from thirteenth century, but only the west end of the original structure remains.

Brekkestø was a harbour of refuge much frequented in ancient times by vessels trading wheat from the Baltic to England: here begins 'Blindleden' (the sheltered channel) which is sheltered by skerries and islands to the eastward, and here ends the coastline of Aust-Agder fylke.

Setesdal—Aust-Agder's Upland

The valley of *Setesdal*, which runs like a wedge into the heights of Haukelifjell, was referred to in 'Historia Norvegiæ' (*ca.* 1175) as being embraced in a law-district 'Telemark with Raabyggelag.'

Eastward of *Byglandsfjord* and in the inner districts of Aust-Agder there exists a scattered population in the remote forest areas. Together with Setesdal and Aaseral they were for centuries administered under 'Raabyggelag'—(a 'raabygger' is one who lives in a 'corner'). No defined boundary was fixed between that district and Agdesiden; in practice the road running eastwards from Evje to Arendal crosses the railway line at Hynnekleiv in Mykland, and there nature and landscape change abruptly and remarkably. This administrative area was dissolved in 1856, when Setesdal was attached to Aust-Agder fylke.

Arendal was ever the town for Setesdal, though after the post-road was built along the bank of the River Otra (or Torridalselv) in the 1840s it was brought nearer to Kristiansand.

This upland area was brought into the timber trade in early days, and the middlemen who bartered corn had things all their own way. In mountain districts there were grumbles in the time of Lofthus (*ca.* 1780) that 'Arendal merchants will not accept our timber, which is virtually our only product,' and therefore they could not procure corn.

The timber is floated down two rivers from heights up to 2,300 feet and a distance of some 150 km.—down Nidelva to Arendal, and Tovdalselva to Tovdalsfjord (just east of Kristiansand). Most of it still finds its way by water, but many lorries are also used; much is delivered to 'The Hunsfoss Paper and Cellulose Factory' north of Kristiansand, but that which comes down Nidelva from Fyresvatn and Nisservatn (which lie inTelemark Fylke) is processed at 'Rygene Trefabrik' near Arendal.

Ascending the Otra valley from Evje one soon arrives at the southern end of the vast Byglandsfjord. Here is one of the most pronounced racial frontiers in all Norway—quite suddenly there is a complete change in racial characteristics, dress, architecture and decoration, language and customs, way of life, cuisine, etc. In Setesdal, customs and ways have been preserved up to quite recently, which are mediæval in character. Their national costume is quaint and particularly colourful. The true 'setesdøler' dwell between the parish boundary dividing Evje from Aardal in the south and the dreaded mountain pass of *Byklestigen;* north of that handicap to communication in bygone days the people of Upper Setesdal have obviously been influenced in blood and speech by their eastern neighbours in Telemark, as also by the Rogaland districts to the west.

At Ose in *Austad* stand two picturesque 'stabbur'—one dating from *ca.* 1640—and higher up the valley one enters *Valle*, whose church lies 760 feet above sea-level. Here, at *Rygnestad*, is the most famous dwelling in Setesdal—a remarkable tower-like building of three storeys and without windows. It was the home of *Vond-Asmund* four centuries ago, relics of whose existence are still to be seen in the upper room, viz.: some tattered leather hangings on which St. George is portrayed fighting with the Dragon, also some Netherlands heraldic devices and scenes with portraits dating from 1560–80. Vond-Asmund is said to have brought them back after fighting in the 'Netherlands War of Freedom,' in which according to local tradition he served under the Duke of Alba. Legend credits him with a violent disposition which led him to commit murder without the slightest provocation. After an absence of seven years, his homecoming coincided with the wedding procession of the fiancée he had left behind. Vond-Asmund snatched her away from the marriage group and bolted with her up the mountainside, where they lived together unmolested for some while. Later they moved to Rygnestad where he built this remarkable 'loft' in the fashion of a fortress. Since he had murdered four of the inhabitants of the valley its people were definitely hostile, and with his bow and arrow he shot from the upper story all and sundry who might be so bold as to approach. He lived there until Death came for him. Since a knife and spoon figure among the relics, he had obviously come in contact with civilized practices unknown in the valley at that time. His descendants still live at the farm in Rygnestad, so it may well be that there is some substance in the legend.

Another strange building called *Kvesteloftet* is said to have been the home of Vilborg—she whose memory has been preserved in one of Pastor Landstad's folksongs.

In ancient days Setesdal's east-west communications were limited to 'Bispeveien,' which runs from the farm of Joreid (to the north of Valle church) eastwards across the mountains to Findalen, and so to Fyresdal in Telemark.

Passing from Valle up Setesdal to Bykle the only approach until the 1870's was up the dreaded '*Byklestigen.*' Many fatal accidents occurred on this rugged passage, beneath which the River Otra runs swiftly through the valley of Valle. That steep and dangerous pass was the line of division of dialects—in Valle the classical Setesdal tongue, in Bykle a mixture with that of Telemark. Bykle church stands 1,600 feet above sea-level, and on both sides of the Otra valley here lie wide stretches of uninhabitable vidde. North of Bykle runs an excellent motor-road which was extended in 1938 across the mountain divide to Haukeligrend in Grungedal, Telemark.

A fascinating old-time occupation on the heights above Valle and Bykle was the trapping of falcons (*falco peregrinus*)—whose value among kings and courtiers was astounding. King John of England (1203) granted a considerable property to a man on condition he provided one falcon from Norway annually, and as late as 1780 Gjellebøl wrote that Dutchmen visited the farm of Breivik in Bykle to snare falcons. They tethered a dove to a post, and, as the falcon struck, the trapper pulled another string attached to a hood on a second post, which enveloped the falcon. After 1560 a number of passes were issued for falcon-trappers in the service of foreign princes, but this all ceased in 1790. On many a Dutch old master can be seen a falcon on the wrist of a knight of other days. Until recently the descendants of a Dutch falcon-trapper named Lieutenant Carolus Kinling were still living in Valle parish.

Gjellebøl wrote of one distressing result of the visit of those Dutchmen, who brought syphilis to the valley. Its ravages among the inhabitants of Setesdal were so disastrous that a State physician was sent up to stem the frightful disease; the blood of the natives was completely non-resistant.

Disputes between Peasants and Citizens

When King Christian IV founded the town of Kristiansand (1641) he granted its citizens monopoly of trade along the entire coast of Agdesiden. This meant that anyone wishing to trade in that area had to take up citizenship in Kristiansand. That decree, however, ran counter to other previous decrees which had granted similar privileges to Tønsberg and other ports in Viken. Tønsberg felt the pinch most, and petitioned the King in 1647. The privileges in the respective royal grants were then argued out before a Royal Commission, which found it impossible to adjudicate and referred the matter to the King himself.

A similar conflict arose between the citizens of Kristiansand and the peasantry, who pleaded they were no longer able to sell timber and its products to strangers and so were unable to pay taxes. The Commission endeavoured to effect a compromise by permitting the peasantry to deal—for a limited period each summer—direct with ships that called at their loading-places. The citizens, however, pressed their claim for their legal privileges, which had wiped out all 'ladesteder' on Agdesiden. Out of this dispute the peasants were granted the valuable concession called *Nedenes Privileges*, under which they could dispose of the products of their forestry direct to Denmark, provided they had first been offered to and declined by the citizens of Kristiansand.

After *Arendal* had received royal permission (1662) to continue temporarily as a timber-loading place until means could be found to transfer its trade to Kristiansand, the peasants were soon raising objections to Arendal merchants acting as middlemen. In 1723 a series of events engendered bitter feelings between the citizens of the newly-created 'town' of Arendal and the peasants in its privileged district. The citizen merchants complained that the peasants were carrying on trade in corn, timber, tar and pitch, etc.—that they built large cutters which they sailed to Denmark, the Baltic, and even to the lands of the west. The Government endeavoured to satisfy both parties to the dispute, but when Arendal was granted its full 'town charter' (1735) Copenhagen learnt that there was great poverty among the peasantry. The King gave his verdict that the ancient '*Nedenes Privileges*' be upheld—'the peasants shall be assisted to earn their livelihood and the citizen his.'

After the imposition of a Danish monopoly of corn imports into southern Norway (1725), the citizens of Arendal exercised a vicious control over its disposal in the coastal and inland districts. It can be no matter for surprise that in years of crop failure the peasantry became rebellious—and there were many such years in the eighteenth century. At length these disputes were referred to the eminent jurist *Henrik Stampe* (1751), who gave judicial condemnation of the whole system of 'privileges,' but ignored the fact that such were essential to enable embryonic towns to progress. In effect, the era of exclusive privileges of both Kristiansand and Arendal came to an end when Stampe's proposals were embodied in modified form in a decree of 1768; the Age of Liberalism had dawned. Yet in spite of Stampe's solution the citizen's monopoly persisted in practice, and it was one of the chief demands of the *Lofthus* Movement in the 1780's that all privileges be abolished. This was effected in 1795, but privileges were reinstituted shortly afterwards. The question was taken up again in the Marcus Thrane (Thraniter) Movement in the 1850's.

The Lofthus Revolt

In Nedenes Amt the people had in the course of time become dependent on the ironmasters and the merchants in the towns. The latter did all in their power to make the peasants their debtors so that they could cut down their forests, and although decrees were issued to limit the usury of the citizens they nevertheless found ways of circumventing them. The ironworks in the province were the main cause for the bad conditions, since their consumption of charcoal was out of all proportion to the size of the forests and to the rewards which the peasants received for their labour. Other liabilities which custom threw upon the labouring class and farmers—such as provision of free transport for officials—proved to be the last straw which tipped the scales into revolt.

A farmer, Kristian Jensson *Lofthus* of Vestre Moland, used this discontent to start a form of rebellion. An illegitimate son of a sailor, he had been adopted by a childless uncle and from him inherited the farm and name of Lofthus. He began well and was awarded a prize by the Trondheim Scientific Society for improvements he had introduced in husbandry. He was, however, of an impetuous, litigious temperament, and gained a measure of popularity by appearing helpful to those in need.

In 1786 Lofthus went to Copenhagen to lay the peasants' complaints before Crown Prince Frederik, in a document with 329 signatures which gave him full Power of Attorney to act on their behalf. The request was that a Commission of impartial men might enquire into the grievance which the country people were nursing against officials, sheriffs and citizens. The authorities noted that Lofthus was illegally calling assemblies, and set the sheriffs after him, whereupon Lofthus surrounded himself with a sort of guard of peasants to avoid surprise. The more the country folk clung to him the greater demands did Lofthus make and, as no Commission of Enquiry was appointed, he set to work to arouse his followers against the government. His meetings were sometimes held openly, but more often in secret, and he travelled far and wide; soon a revolt became imminent.

The Stiftamtmann decided to secure the person of Lofthus, but the platoon of soldiers sent to his farm found him absent, as he had jumped from an attic window and taken refuge in the forests. He then collected a force of some 300 men in Raabyggelaget and marched to Lillesand. There the Stiftamtmann addressed the gathering, and two peasants implored that Lofthus might be free from arrest and given a pass to travel to Copenhagen; they represented the burden of taxation as intolerable. The 'ting' at Lillesand passed off without disturbance and the Stiftamtmann later granted Lofthus a pass for his Copenhagen journey. He departed accompanied by thirty men, but on arrival in Helsingborg heard that plans had been made to lock him up in a fortress at Copenhagen. Some of his followers then proceeded to that city to obtain a safe conduct for him, and one was made out for a stay of six weeks there. Meanwhile, out of fear that the Swedish authorities would hand him over, Lofthus returned home.

The authorities took matters seriously and the commandant at Kristiansand at once sent soldiers to arrest him. Then began a hunt by officials and sheriffs, and great fears were held that Lofthus and his 'mountaineers' were about to invade the towns. In both Kristiansand and Arendal there was a state of panic. It is said that no fewer than 2,000 followers gathered round Lofthus, a movement which induced the authorities to negotiate and come to an agreement under which Lofthus should be free from arrest for five weeks provided he did nothing illegal. The government appears to have wished to do justice to the peasants; Lofthus was given a new safe conduct, provided he appeared in Copenhagen within two months, and a Commission of Enquiry was appointed. Lofthus had, however, no confidence in the safe conduct from the authorities, so he took refuge in Telemark where the Stiftamtmann called upon the military for support. But that province was already alight with resisters to taxation: several peasants in Øvre Telemark had taken part in the disturbances during December.

Three members of the Commission of Enquiry began hearing complaints in January 1787, and on the 11th of that month Lofthus came to Kristiansand where he objected to certain of its members, who were changed. Six weeks earlier Bishop Hagerup had reported to the Treasury: 'The condition of the people is deplorable. There is shortage of food for both human beings and cattle, lack of provisions of foodstuffs and money to buy same . . . . it will soon be intolerable as crop failures, high cost of living and distressing poverty stifle the countryside.'

The attitude of the Commission to Lofthus was two-faced—it regarded him as a dangerous criminal, and had found the Kristiansand districts peaceful and loyal to the Crown. Two leading authorities concocted a plan to seize Lofthus which was effected on 15th March in Lillesand, whence he was removed in frightful weather to Horten and later in an armed vessel to Akershus. There he was chained to a block in the barracks.

On the arrest of Lofthus his followers retaliated by seizing a bailiff, and when the Stiftamtmann demanded his release unharmed, they replied they first wanted to see the royal order for Lofthus's arrest. Soldiers then marched out of Kristiansand to free the bailiff, but having done this they had to return hurriedly to Kristiansand as it was reported that the Setesdøler were threatening that town.

The government at once remedied the worst features that had caused the revolt, but the investigations into the affair of Lofthus dragged on. Not until the fifth anniversary (15th March, 1792) was judgment pronounced—that Lofthus himself should suffer imprisonment for life in irons, whilst thirteen of his followers were sentenced to up to three years of the same imprisonment. Lofthus died in prison on 13th June, 1797.

The original charges levelled against Lofthus (1782) were that he dealt in corn and other commodities to the detriment of Arendal's privileges. The ancient Nedenes Privileges were claimed by its peasants as late as 1820, though the Storting had put an end to them in 1818. The new liberalistic order took a different view to that of the absolute monarchs.

CHAPTER XV

VEST-AGDER FYLKE

Kristiansand

KING Christian IV lay at Flekkerøy (June 1635) in his vessel 'Christian's Ark,' and gave orders for the stone fort there to be known as *Christiansø*. It was to be erected on Gammeløen. This small island—a couple of hundred meters either way, no more than 15 meters high—was sometimes called Slottsholmen, then Christiansø, in modern times the usual name is Gammeløen (the old island). The island is situated in the western approach to the harbour of Flekkerøy—a port which had for long been frequented by skippers of ships of many nations. The State Council agreed that its position made it the obvious key to both the North Sea and Baltic. Christian informed the Netherlands through diplomatic channels that he had taken this step 'in order to protect their subjects against piratical attacks.'

King Christian took counsel (1639) with his 'lensherre' on Agdesiden—Palle Rosenkrantz—as to where the new town he proposed to found should be sited, and two years later, 5th July, 1641, a royal charter was granted to *Christiansand*, 'at the place in Nedenes Len in Our Kingdom of Norway which is called Sanden.' At the same time the King granted the two estates of Grim and Eg as a 'bymark' (townfields) for Kristiansand.

The King's purpose was military-strategical, even as had been his previous attention to Flekkerøy's defence. This attitude was emphasized when the foundations of a Norwegian standing army were laid by a royal decree issued only five days after the granting of Kristiansand's Charter; indeed that town has ever been a military base. The King spent some days at Flekkerøy (May 1644) when the 'Hannibal War' was raging.

Whilst the Dutch-English War was being fought out (1652–54), Flekkerøy was put in a state of defence under the command of *Jørgen Bjelke*, since Frederik III feared that Cromwell 'might wish to seize the fort and harbour in order to prey upon Dutch shipping trading with Norway, Denmark and the Baltic.' When all danger from Cromwell had passed, the fort of Christiansø was abandoned, and a new fort named *Frederiksholm* built on an island further up the channel which could command both approaches. Frederiksholm was completed in 1658 and, although never brought up to date, stood until 1807. During the Dano-German war of 1848 the forts at Christiansø and Fredriksholm were somewhat restored, and also during the Crimean war small garrisons were stationed there. The two islands were definitely evacuated as military points of support in 1871.

The forts around Christiansand had never been in combat until the 9th of April, 1940. The old forts at Flekkerøy harbour never shot a cannon except during manœuvres and as salutes to passing ships. We have preserved the accounts of ammunitions at these forts, so we know the names of most of the Dutch and British marine ships and captains coming into Christiansand harbour during the second half of the seventeenth and the whole of the eighteenth century. Unarmed merchant ships were not so greeted (except when they carried cannon and saluted first). But the accounts inform us of many convoys having their meeting place here during the troublous times in western Europe.

The pivot of defence on Agdesiden was gradually transferred to Kristiansand, and in 1672 the town fort of *Christiansholm* was erected, much of which survives. The first fort to be constructed on *Odderøya* was built shortly afterwards and, still more important, the headquarters of 'The Norwegian Coastal Galley Fleet' was transferred from Fredrikstad to Kristiansand in 1686. A dockyard was built, called 'Christiansand's Søekvipage,' and both warships and galleys constructed; in both the Gyldenløve War (1675–79) and Great Northern War (1709–20) it played a major role. During the exciting events of the latter period Kristiansand was Norway's principal naval station, and Tordenskiold himself was a frequent visitor. After the Peace of 1720 it faded out as a naval base; eventually the dockyard was abandoned.

Kristiansand was primarily a military town which was, however, converted by artificial means into the administrative centre —military, ecclesiastical, and civil—for all Sørlandet. Previous to its foundation the 'lensherre' at Nedenes Kongsgaard was the supreme authority over all Agdesiden, until he was ordered to transfer his headquarters to the neighbourhood of the new fortress. Palle Rosenkrantz set up his administration staff (1637) in the recently completed 'kongsgaard' at *Oddernes* (Otranes) to supervise the districts of Nedenes, Mandal and Lista; in 1655 Oddernes became an adjunct of Kristiansand, instead of vice versa. Transition from 'lensherre' to 'civil servant' (stiftamtmann) in 1661 under absolute monarchy, caused many difficulties, but after that year both civil and military control were vested in the 'stiftamtmann.' This was a triumph for the bourgeoisie over the nobles, though any noticeable change was long in being felt in Agdesiden, since it was a distant province from which the organs of state control lay very remote.

A new 'charter of privileges' was granted to Kristiansand (1662): under these all trade was to be concentrated in that town, except timber exports, which might continue to be handled at Arendal, Risør and Mandal 'until means can be found to bring them to Kristiansand.' By these privileges such places as Flekkefjord were to be deprived of all trade, though the privileges were not enforced by Kristiansand's citizens beyond limits that suited their own purposes. Against interference from all *other towns*, both peasantry and citizens adopted an united front.

According to Bishop Erik Pontoppidan (*ca.* 1750) it had been Christian IV's intention to transfer the See of Stavanger to Kristiansand. The mayor of the latter town wrote to the Treasury in Copenhagen (1682): 'Stavanger is a town in decay,' and pleaded for the transfer of its See to his town. In response King Christian V issued an instruction to Stiftamtmann Rosenkrantz and to Bishop Jersin of Stavanger that this was to be effected—that the church at Kristiansand should become the cathedral, and that Stavanger's chapter and cathedral school were also to be moved there. Thus it comes about that 6th May, 1682 is regarded in Kristiansand as one of its principal anniversaries, second only to that of its foundation day (5th July, 1641).

Begun in 1685, the first cathedral was in the style of Vor Frelsers at Christiania: when it burnt down in 1734 a loss of tradition was bewailed. The loss of its second cathedral by fire in 1880 was an even greater tragedy—many residents 'felt its disappearance as a personal sorrow.'

As in the rest of Europe, witch-hunting was indulged in during mid-seventeenth century. Six witches perished together in the flames here as late as 1670, one of whom confessed she had flown to Copenhagen in the guise of the Devil holding a glass, and had poured poison into the ear of Kristiansand's mayor who was there on official business. By 1729, however, the ridicule Holberg had poured on such superstition had penetrated public opinion and it was possible for a resident to write: 'When those six witches were burnt together all the witches in the whole world perished in the flames, for since that time I have not read of any trolldom and hereafter there will be none.'

After 1690 foreigners began to settle in Kristiansand, which was granted religious freedom, like Fredrikstad.

A great fire at Kristiansand (1734) was a serious blow to its citizens as well as to the peasantry in its privileged district of Vest-Agder. Disputes between the bourgeoisie of the town and its 'tied' peasants were acrid and incessant all through the eighteenth century. Citizen monopoly in the timber and corn trades brought hardships to the peasants, and since in 1688 the timber trade up the valleys of Fyresdal and Nissedal in Telemark had been placed by decree under Kristiansand, the entire peasantry over a very wide area were hostile to the citizens of that town.

Yet the latter built up an export trade, and shipping flourished after the fire (1734) until the close of the Seven Years War (1763). Then came difficult years until the American Rebellion brought good times once more, and Kristiansand—with State assistance—became a considerable import town. Nicolai Wergeland wrote later that his town thrived in war but shrivelled in peace—that it might find its parallel in Algiers or Jomsborg. Welhaven satirically described Kristiansand as a town which 'lived honourably upon wrecks'—an expression used earlier by Holberg in 'Peder Paars' about the islanders of Anholt in the Kattegat.

When King Christian VI visited Agdesiden in 1733 with his old German mother, his diary was kept by a tiresome pietist who shared that austere king's severe outlook on life, so different from the jaunty tone of Frederik IV's diarist. The King had noticed the plague of beggars, which grew to alarming proportions after the Kristiansand fire of 1734, when numbers tramped the countryside begging for food. King Christian ordered the Stiftamtmann to take steps to deal with the problem, but it was not until 1782 that a rational system of 'care for the poor' was introduced. Bishop Eiler Hagerup, who had been priest at Arendal in his younger years (1756–73), made a personal appeal to the inhabitants, and a 'Tugt og Manufactur Huus' (Correction and Workhouse) was opened at Kristiansand in 1789. In theory it was to be self-supporting, but that soon proved to be an illusion.

Many coastal districts in Norway were plagued with *syphilis* in the eighteenth century. A Danish 'apoteker' from Holbæk came to Arendal with a secret concoction for its cure, which was shown by the primitive methods of analysis then available to be possibly a danger to life. This aroused the indignation of the Danish authorities, who issued an edict (1782) prohibiting the practice of 'quackery' without agreement by a physician.

Once in the course of its existence Kristiansand had promise of a brilliant cultural future. Bishop Gunnerus approached Struensee—during the short period of 'omnipotence' enjoyed by that misguided liberal adventurer (1771)—with the suggestion that a University of Norway be founded in that town. Gunnerus proposed moving 'Videnskabsselskabet' (The Scientific Society) there from Trondheim: himself to take up residence with eleven professors. Struensee, however, threw over the proposal, otherwise Kristiansand might well have become the University Town. It boasted both a Dramatic and a Musical Society as early as 1787.

During the early years of the Napoleonic Wars the defences of the town of Kristiansand, which then housed some 4,800 souls, came up for review by the State, but nothing was done about them. So when Captain Stopford in the battleship 'Spencer' anchored off Frederiksholm on 11th September, 1807—with a frigate and gunboat in company—no counteraction was possible. The commander of the land defences, Stiftamtmann Thygeson, sent a defiant reply to Stopford's menacing letter but no force was available to repel the English landing on Flekkerøy, which they plundered in piratical fashion. Then they blew up the fortifications on Fredriksholm fort, which had been abandoned as a fortress three years previously, but still served as a storehouse for various military effects. Total loss of lives in this action was three British marines and one lieutenant who were sent ashore to see why the explosion was delayed. Possibly the intention was to strike terror into the people of Kristiansand. The effect produced was, however, the contrary, and when more than two thousand men were posted to resist a British landing, and a flotilla of gunboats opened an effective fire, the British force withdrew.

When the British attempted a landing at Rossvaag in Lyngdal, several women dressed in military uniforms were said to have scared the enemy, though it seems more probable that 150 men in a number of small boats were responsible for the British abandoning the attempt.

In 1808 a brisk action took place off Kristiansand between the British brig 'Seagull' and the Norwegian 'Lougen.' The former was so severely battered that she struck her flag, and was towed into Kristiansand by 'Lougen.'

* * * * *

A Prize Court sat at Kristiansand during the 'Privateer' period following 1807, when many a prize was brought in with holds full of valuable cargo. Fortunes were made by local capitalists, who bought at auction at knock-out prices: occasionally buyers attended from as far away as Copenhagen.

At long last Odderøya was strongly fortified under the threat of a great danger: it was garrisoned again during the Crimean War to uphold the neutrality of Norway. When next danger was at hand (1914) it was reported that: 'the sole defence of the fortress is a padlock on the gate, together with the raised axe on the Royal Arms over the gateway.' Yet a serious warning had been given by King Oscar II when he visited Kristiansand in 1891. He drew attention to the long period of uninterrupted peace enjoyed since 1814, and warned the citizens that they had a duty to defend their independence—'especially in the case of a town of such strategic importance as Kristiansand occupies in the scheme of national defence.'

The '*Privateer*' Period (1807–1814), coupled with the *Licence* trade (1809–1812), led to swindles, speculation, bribery and corruption on such a scale that Schweigaard wrote of it in 1840: 'town property, ships, forests, saw-mills—all attained values which later caused violent upheavals in the economic life of the country.' He continued: 'whether it would be right to desire a renewal of such conditions is extremely doubtful.' As we all know, such conditions were repeated in recent years—and with equally disastrous consequences.

Kristiansand was a town of contrasts following the adoption of the Eidsvoll Constitution (1814)—on the one hand hunger and want, on the other song and dance. It became a resort of pedlars, paupers and bankrupts.

By 1824 Norways' shipping and trade attained a considerable measure of independence. The enormous development of productivity in the workshops of the world called for increased tonnage to transport goods. New ships were built, and their routes covered the Seven Seas. After England had repealed her navigation acts (1849) free trade and competition made their effects felt in the shipping world: by 1853 Norway occupied fifth place among the maritime nations. During the Crimean War ships brought home fortunes, until freights dropped disastrously in 1856; slumps the world over led to many bankruptcies, and Kristiansand fell into the international melting-pot for the first time in its history. Slumps continued to affect economic life at the close of every decade until the outbreak of the Second World War—that of 1929 being by far the most serious.

During the First World War speculation was wildly indulged in, and swindles were the order of the day. The peak was reached when the vast British American Nickel Corporation was acquired, which cost the citizens of Kristiansand a pretty penny. Post-war bankruptcies became a spate after 1921.

'Rationalism' had its first outburst in Kristiansand through its Bishop, Peder Hansen (1798–1804); schools and lecture-rooms were fields of his activities. Reaction to this attitude to life was also strongest in that town, where Hans Nielsen Hauge had his most fruitful sphere. It was here that he bought a printing press which was 'under royal patronage,' and published several banned pamphlets. He even got started a paper-mill at Fennefoss in Hornnes to furnish his printing press with paper. This was a shortlived enterprise, as it was difficult to get enough rags for the making of paper, and the financial foundation was unsound.

On Dronningensgate No. 21 is a brass plate: 'Here *Henrik Wergeland* was born 17th June, 1808': many of his verses and the first edition of his celebrated account of the Lofthus Movement were printed in Kristiansand. Abildgaard, later a leading member of the Thraniter Movement, edited a local paper in 1850.

Kristiansand was reared as a 'cuckoo in the nest,' which was artificially fed and, as it were, kept alive in an oxygen tent by its founder Christian IV and his grandson, the viceroy Ulrik Frederik Gyldenløve. The old king planned and laid out the town in rectangles—its main streets running between the harbour on the west and the River Otra on the east. Its ancient history was enacted at *Oddernes* (Otranes) just beyond the city boundary, where stands a stone church from the eleventh century. Runes on a bautastein in the churchyard read 'Eyvind, godson of Olav the Saint, caused this church to be built on his odel land.' *Eyvind Urarhorn* was killed in the Orkneys (1019), and Olav (the saint) was at Oddernes shortly after his death: he stood godfather to the young Eyvind.

Some 25 km. from Kristiansand on the banks of the Topdal River lies one of Sørlandet's largest estates in the parish of *Tveit*, where stands a church of equal age to that at Oddernes. *Boen* is the manor house whose fine building was completed in 1812; it has been frequented by fishermen ever since the Bronze Age. Peder Clausson wrote (*ca.* 1580): 'Through this valley runs a large river full of salmon . . .', where as many as 400 large fish were caught daily—English fishermen leased it through much of the nineteenth century.

In 1753 Boen and its fishery was bought by an Irishman, Edward Smythe, who had by then become 'citizen and merchant in Kristiansand': it was believed that he was a nobleman who had fled his homeland after a duel. He made a great deal of money, owned shipyards and cranes at Kristiansand, several saw-mills and ships, and then was all but ruined through shipwrecks and town fires. So he left Norway in 1765 and sold his holdings to his sister Margaret Smythe and her husband, who was a ship captain and merchant from Viborg in Jutland named Arctander. When the latter died in 1775, his widow retained Boen till her death in 1801, when it passed to *Daniel Isaachsen*, who owned the pretty estate of *Kjos* (see p. 170) just west of Kristiansand—for he had married Margaret Smythe's granddaughter.

It was Daniel Isaachsen who at Boen built the present delightful manor house during the 'golden years,' but owing to outbreak of war completion was delayed until 1812, and Isaachsen died early in the following year before he had moved in. His capable widow continued to beautify house and garden, which was laid out to English design. Their daughter married a Hegermann, in which name ownership continued until 1938.

On the river bank below Boen lies the aerodrome of *Kjevik*, a spot which was much in favour with the advisers of Christian IV as the site of his proposed town of Kristiansand.

A short distance below Kjevik a high-level bridge across Topdalsella was completed in 1956. This has brought Kristiansand very near its aerodrome, and also appreciably closer to Lillesand and the other coastal towns of Aust-Agder fylke.

A successful member of the commercial aristocracy who accumulated capital during the good years after 1750 was Bernt Holm (1765–1829), who bought the ancient estate of Eg. His chief interest was, however, centred round the house he named *Gimle* which he built in Lundsia, i.e. the east bank of the River Otra. The name he drew from Old Norse mythology which made Gimle the new heaven that should arise after Ragnarokk. Completed in 1807, it lies on a slope down to Torridalselva, with views over Kristiansand and the fjord. It was the scene of a magnificent wedding feast for Bernt Holm's daughter, Petronelle, when she married Major Arenfeldt, of Sæby Castle near Frederikshavn in Jutland.

When Eg was sold to the State for a lunatic asylum (1877), the wealthy Arenfeldt of that time divided his year between his mansions at Sæby and Gimle. His daughter, Ingertha (died 1948) married an Omdal, and in the name of *Arenfeldt-Omdal* Gimle is held till this day. The Germans installed themselves for five long years: there was a grand celebration of 'liberation' here at Christmas 1945, when an old-time feast was held, with servants in the liveries of other days, and dances which the older people present had enjoyed in the days of their youth.

Some 4 km. west of Kristiansand lay the pretty little estate of *Kjos*, which is now (1956) being developed as a 'garden city.' It was acquired by *Daniel Isaachsen* in 1784, who at once brought over from Peterhead and Aberdeen a capable stockman, together with twelve farm hands, a gardener who laid out the park, and two Scottish women to spin wool, knit stockings, etc. They brought with them many farm implements unknown in Norway —as also cattle and sheep from Britain and pigs from Ireland. Then Daniel engaged the services of a potter from England, after having sent a sample of local clay there for a report on its suitability for the 'earthenware' he proposed to produce. Then followed a miller to construct a corn-mill by a waterfall close to the house at Kjos, to a design previously unknown in Norway, with Scottish millstones which first removed the husks of oats and then ground the grain into fine or coarse flour as required. Daniel Isaachsen was obviously a man of energy and resource: the attractive manor house he and his wife built at *Boen* survives as a happy memorial of the days of Napoleon.

It was also in those times (1797) that an Irishman named *Robert Major* founded the 'Kongsgaard Tannery' in Kristiansand, which still operates though there is no longer a 'Major' in the firm. His son, Herman Wedel Major, made the first Norwegian law to provide for the insane; he was an outstanding alienist. With him came over the first '*Coward*'—a name which is linked to vast undertakings in production of 'deals' and timber processing, as also to the initiation of electricity undertakings.

At the seaward end of the Valley of Mandalen lies *Mandal*, Norway's most southerly town and the oldest on Agdesiden. Its earliest name was 'Buane'—*alias* 'The Danish warehouses in Mandalen'—no doubt due to the fact that *Landskrona* (on Øresund) was granted salmon fishing privileges here (*ca.* 1400), and retained its economic hold in Mandal until the seventeenth century. Peder Clausson wrote that Landskronians came each year to buy salmon, which they sold in Lübeck, and supplied Mandalen with its import requirements from overseas. The Germans, led by one Morten Baad, tried to oust Landskrona in 1553, and the merchants of that town continued to voice complaints regarding interlopers until the close of the sixteenth century. The rancorous German schoolmaster who wrote 'Den norske So' (1580) chastened Mandalians for their dissipated way of life.

The later site of 'Buane' (de danske boder i Mandalen) cannot be older than first half of seventeenth century, since the river changed its course (*ca.* 1625), and as recently as 1640 the Customs House was transferred from Snig to 'de danske boder.' The foundation of Kristiansand (1641) occasioned great loss to Landskrona, whose privileges ceased entirely at Mandal when Skaane passed to Swedish sovereignty (1658). Nevertheless the old name 'de danske boder og Kleven' was in use until late in the eighteenth century.

Mandal's progress was halted by the foundation of Kristiansand (1641) and even after 1690 its merchants had to pay 2 per cent. of value of exports to the 'royal' city in order to be free from the obligation to reside within its town limits. The concessions granted to Arendal and Risør in 1723 did not apply to Mandal, which was not freed from Kristiansand's stranglehold until 1779.

Jean Bart, the French naval hero, put in at Mandal in 1696, after having defeated a Dutch fleet sent to intercept a convoy of vessels laden with corn which Jean Bart was to have protected on its voyage from southern Norwegian ports to France.

The grand old man of Mandal was *Tørris Christensen Nedenes*, who was of a Danish family and married a Danish girl—he made a fortune in the troubles around the year 1700, and owned the estate of *Halsaa*, which covered the western part of modern Mandal. He made a personal loan to King Frederik IV when that monarch visited Mandal (1704); one of his functions was that of a glorified pawnbroker, an occupation which enabled him to acquire many gold and silver treasures and elegant furniture brought from Holland during that age of 'dignity.' He mounted cannon, to keep pirates from entering the harbour, at a spot which has ever since been known as 'Kastellet,' and from his own resources satisfied the sum demanded from a Swedish warship during the reign of Karl XII for not devastating Mandal. Tørris was known as 'kongen i Mandal,' and Danish families controlled the life of the little place so completely that native-born Norwegians were given no opportunity to advance in the social scale. Some patrician houses yet remain to recall traditions of its prosperous past—it owed success to trade with the Dutch, and the influence of that nation is prominent in the buildings that survive, since no other town on Agdesiden has retained such obvious links with the Netherlands. A traveller in 1799 wrote: 'the houses are jammed together so tightly that a careless pipe-smoker at any open window could spit into his neighbour's parlour.' There was a considerable emigration to Holland.

A fascinating old building is 'Skrivergaarden,' which was erected *ca.* 1770 in Scottish sandstone after the style of a Scottish mansion, and with a Scotsman named Johnstone as master-mason.

Bad times came to the port after 1807. As an additional blow came the great fire of 1810. In despair at conditions a merchant named *Salvesen* fitted out two pirate schooners called 'Le petit diable' and 'Prøven'; their dividends were, however, but meagre. The family of Salvesen lived on in Mandal, but one branch emigrated to Scotland, where at Leith and Grangemouth they founded shipping lines which carried on a considerable trade with Norway. One of its scions became 'Lord-Advocate for Scotland' in the 1920's, with the title of 'Lord.' He retained a summer house in Mandal which the local people affectionately called 'The lord's house.'

Mandal was the birthplace of two world-famous Norwegian artists—*Adolf Tidemand* (1814–71) whose canvases surely delight the eye of 'everyman,' and *Gustav Vigeland* whose sculpture is outstanding in the twentieth century. His works in Trognerparken, Oslo, call forth condemnation from a section of the public—and admiration from perhaps a similar proportion.

A short distance westward from Mandal lies the Valley of *Audnedal.* At the church of Valle at the seaward end of that valley hangs the portrait of *Peder Clausson Friis*, with this legend beneath: 'Born Egersund 1545—priest in Sör-Audnedal 1566—died 1614, aged 69.' This was painted by Peter Reimers shortly before Peder Clausson's death. He had himself rebuilt his church in 1591, but that structure was, alas, demolished (1795) to be replaced by the present church. At Breime, in Sør-Audnedal parish, *Gustav Vigeland* built a summer house close to the shore where he could watch the breakers surging to and fro—he was by nature a restless soul and surely saw his own reflection in the fury of the surf.

On an isthmus at *Spangereid* stands an ancient stone church from the thirteenth century—indeed some experts give the date as *ca.* 1075. Its peninsula is *Lindesnes*, on whose extreme point stands the famous lighthouse at the most southerly spot on Norway's mainland. Some 4 km. northwest of that cape lie the islands of *Seløyene*, so frequently mentioned in the sagas as harbours of refuge for vessels and fleets sailing in or out of the Skagerak, where they awaited favourable winds for their change of course along the coast. Seløyene have ever been densely populated—their centre being the little town of *Korshavn.*

Peder Clausson Friis called *Vanse* stone church (thirteenth century) 'a lovely building and the largest rural church in the diocese of Stavanger.' Peder knew it well since he was the object of an attack there by a turbulent priest named Storch—one of whose colleagues had trumped up a charge against him that he 'lived in sin with a female slut named Marine.' Stavanger chapter deprived Storch of his living (1594), whereupon his son and stepson vied with each other to step into his office. Peder Clausson, as archdeacon, endeavoured to arbitrate between them, and it was then that one of them attacked him. The Diocesan Council expelled both priests from their diocese.

One priest at Vanse practised 'the black arts,' which earned him the soubriquet 'Wise Paal.' Many tales survive concerning his communion with occult forces, whilst his generosity to all and sundry led him to give away church collections as well as his own boots—so that on one occasion he ascended the pulpit barefoot.

At the close of the eighteenth century two priests—father and son named Bugge—functioned here. They were both 'Moravians,' and Bishop Claus Pavels stated that half the populace of *Lista* were of that persuasion. The younger Bugge became Bishop of Trondheim, where he died in 1849. *Fritzner*—author of the great work 'Det gamle norske sprog'—was priest at Vanse until 1877, when he transferred to Christiania in order to pilot his massive volume through the press.

Between Lyngdalsfjord and Fedefjord lies the peninsula of *Lista*—surrounded by salt water on three sides, and famous for its yield of rich remains from the Bronze Age. Its praises have been sung by Bertha Koren and Thomas Krag: another of its sons, Bishop Claus Pavels, took a gloomier view of its attractions when he wrote in his famous autobiography: 'Its scenery does not evoke a desire to indulge in poetry since the district, though fertile, is far from beautiful! I have never liked it.' Near the ancient stone church of Vanse lies *Huseby*, the site of the 'hall' of a thane in Viking times, with a wide prospect over land and sea. It may be that Huseby was the 'capital' of that 'Kingdom in south-west Norway' which Harald Fairhair annexed after the Battle of Hafrsfjord. Beint Kolbeinsson of Lista was King Inge I's sysselmann in Lista until killed by Sigurd Slembe (1138), and at Huseby stood one of the 'royal chapels'—dedicated to St. Laurence—during the reign of Haakon V.

When Otto Stigsson held Lista 'len' in 1542, he complained that Scottish pirates plundered the neighbourhood, and proposed the establishment of a 'town' to provide man-power at hand to repel pirates.

Povel Juel, the notorious traitor, lived at Huseby while amtmann here (1712–20): he was executed at Copenhagen (1723).

The town of *Farsund*, with its two outer harbours of Eigvaag and Lushavn lying some 4 km. distant, was laid out within the estate of Huseby, which eventually came into the possession of the family of *Lund*. They laid the foundations of Farsund's period of prosperity, and Jochum Brinck Lund flourished exceedingly here during the 'fat' years around 1805: his ancestor was a shipwrecked Danish skipper who married a local girl (1688). Jochum built a magnificent timber house for his sons called *Husan*, and laid out a splendid garden around it. He must have been most enterprising, since not only did his vessels fish as far away as Iceland—indeed, he started an institute of fishery research—but he founded dye-works, using as raw material a moss which grew in a near-by marsh. Those works were bought up by a Glasgow firm of dyers. Old Jochum died in 1807 just as every thing slumped, but shipwrecks continued a good source of income and privateering brought useful dividends. On one occasion a Farsund privateer slipped into a Scottish port, cut the cables of a large English ship and brought her back in triumph to Farsund. The firm of Lund faded out in 1837. A disastrous fire in 1901 destroyed the entire town except the grand old house of 'Husan' which was spared owing to its spacious garden; alas, it was burnt to the ground during the German occupation, so that Farsund is in its entirety a twentieth-century town. Its most famous son was *Eilert Lund Sundt*—the social statistician—who died as priest at Eidsvoll in 1875.

Kvinesdalen, which reaches saltwater at the head of the deep Fedefjord, was the home of many prominent characters during the Saga Period, notably 'Kjotve the wealthy,' and the skald 'Tjodolv of Hvin.' A son of the valley in later times was *Stig Bagge*, whose father addressed a letter to the king 'from his house Rafos' (1543). Peder Clausson tells a gruesome tale of Stig's methods in putting down a revolt (see p. 140): he remained the 'bogey-man' in the neighbourhood for years to come; when anybody offended the susceptibilities of the people they used to call out: 'You are not Stig Bagge.' As a sea-captain he was caught on Walcheren, and condemned to a gruesome death as a spy. When 'lensherre' in Lista he lived at his ancestral home, Eikeland, in Kvinesdal.

A priest in the valley was arraigned before the Stavanger chapter because he had attached to himself a female without going through the formalities of engagement and publishing banns. After she had lived with him for some time he sent her home 'because her legs were bad.'

The westernmost town in Vest-Agder is *Flekkefjord*, lying on an arm of the deep Fedefjord. It was a 'ladested' from early times, being mentioned as a 'town' as long ago as 1580. Twice was it sentenced to extinction by royal decree, but its sturdy inhabitants ignored the orders and continued to trade without coming under complete control of 'royal' Kristiansand. In 1760 Flekkefjord petitioned Frederik V to grant a 'Town charter,' and to permit its renaming as 'Frederiksfjord.' At that date several ships were sailing from its harbour and many sailors had their homes in the little town—which by 1805 had a lively trade with Holland and England.

Flekkefjord's exports were mainly fish until the herring deserted the coast in 1838, but members of the family of *Beer* kept its prosperity flourishing over a long period. Jens Henrik Beer (1731–1808) went to school in Holland, and then carried on a large trade with Scotland in timber, bringing malt and flour as return cargoes. During the French wars he bought Scottish manufactured goods and sold them in France, where he sailed freely under the Danish flag. Having benefited himself as well as Scotland he was made a 'freeman' of Montrose, and thus became a symbol of trade between Norway and Scotland. His grandson *Anders Beer* (1801–63) was educated in France and speculated in herring and ship-building until the former left the coast (1838). He then founded a tanyard and brought three experts from England: he was the first in Norway to use oak bark instead of birch, and South American hides instead of Norwegian. By 1866 five tanneries were operating in Flekkefjord, and a large export of leather was going to Sweden. After his death the tanning industry began to fade away: a street is named after him. His younger brother J. H. Beer studied in England and introduced new agricultural practices in Fedefjord, where he employed a Scottish foreman for many years. From his farm at Øye he indulged in forestry on a large scale, planting larch, pine and deciduous trees previously unknown in Kvinesdal.

A picturesque corner of Flekkefjord is '*Hollenderbyen*'—a name which recalls the days of lively trade with that country.

Sirdalen is the northernmost valley in Vest-Agder, and at the north end of its long, narrow lake—Siredalsvatn—lies the village of Tonstad. On the desolate heights above the upper valley, falcons used to be trapped by Dutchmen a couple of centuries ago; one of them is said to have bought an island in the lake for 'an old hat,' which recalls the old 'tag':

> In matters of commerce the fault of the Dutch
> Is giving too little and asking too much.

The railway from Flekkefjord to Stavanger climbs tortuously as up goat tracks, with no fewer than forty-six tunnels before reaching Egersund—and thus we pass out of Vest-Agder and out of Sørlandet, into Rogaland.

PART V

ROGALAND

CHAPTER XVI

ROGALAND

Rogaland in Pre-history

STONE AGE MAN was roaming over Rogaland possibly as early as 4500 B.C.: an 'armoury' from that time has been unearthed at *Bømlo* immediately north of the fylke boundary. Bone hunting weapons from the later Stone Age (*ca.* 3000 B.C.) were found in a cave at Viste in Jæren, and at nearby Aamøy two fishes were cut upon a rock. Bronze Age man later superimposed two ships upon the fish which form part of an extensive 'hellerristning.' A considerable deposit of flint implements, including no fewer than twenty-seven flint daggers, was found on the island of Karmøy, whilst Jæren has yielded numerous amber ornaments. The latter originated in Jutland, whereas those found around Trondheimsfjord came from Prussia—an indication of lines of communication in the very-long-ago.

During the *Early Bronze Age* (*ca.* 1500 B.C.) impressive barrows were thrown up at Lista, Jæren and Karmøy over dead Norwegian chieftains: these make those areas the classic districts of the Bronze Age.

The technique of smelting *iron* reached Jæren from Germany at an early date, and created an upheaval in the life of Norway. Rogaland provided the scene of its most flourishing development, particularly in Jæren, which had been the most prosperous part of the country during the entire Bronze Age. It is a remarkable fact that although the most northerly find from the Bronze Age was as far north as 68°, those of the *Early Iron Age* are all south of 60°; Rogaland escaped the worst effects of the drastic change in climate which elsewhere eclipsed agricultural and community life between *ca.* 700 B.C. and A.D. 200. 'Flaghaugen,' close to Avaldsnes church, is an immense barrow from the Roman Iron Age; close by stands the 21-foot long 'bautastein' called 'Virgin Mary's Needle.' Five 'bautastein' from the same period stand at Norheim across Karmsound; forming an equilateral triangle they are locally referred to as 'the five foolish virgins.'

Foundations of nine dwellings have been excavated at Ferkingstad on Karmøy, the largest of which was 50 yards in length. This was surely a 'kongsgaard' during the *Migration Period* (A.D. 400–600), at which time much gold reached Rogaland, having been plundered by the Gothic tribes invading Italy. Rogaland obtained the largest share and undoubtedly enjoyed a high standard of living—possibly due to flourishing trade and shipping. Other finds from the Migration Period include an animal brooch (*ca.* A.D. 400) at Ogna in Jæren, and a quantity of glass, mostly of provincial Roman origin. From Vest-Agder comes the *Snartemo* sword, whose hilt is covered in gold foil and richly embellished; also a magnificent beaker of Rhine glass from the sixth century.

Norway was peopled by folk of various origins; more conservative conditions ruled in Trøndelag and the Opplands, it was the west and south coasts which were most affected by the movements of hordes of tribes from the Continent during the Migration Period. It is probable that at some date during the *Merovingian Period* (A.D. 600–800) an invading horde conquered and colonized the coastal districts between Stavanger and Arendal (see p. 129). The evicted 'ryger' were driven into Ryfylke and Haugaland; indeed, whenever Snorre mentions Rogaland he refers solely to the area north and east of Boknfjord. Ryfylke continued to maintain close contact with the Franks, at all events until the beginning of the Viking Age (*ca.* A.D. 800).

The Viking Age (A.D. 800–1000)

The descendants of the 'ryger' who originally peopled Ryfylke are forever associated with the settlement of *Iceland*, which was given its name by *Floke Vilgerdson*, the 'rogalending' who sailed away from Ryvarden (Smørsund, on the northern limit of Rogaland) with three ravens to give him his course. Floke was the very first settler, but was so busy fishing that he neglected to assemble fodder for his cattle, which all died of starvation during his first winter. He was back in Rogaland in the spring, but returned to make a fresh start. An entire colony from Agdesiden settled down in Tjorsaadalen after Helge-the-Slim had asked Tor for an oracle as to where he should land. Helge took possession of all Eyafjord, and 'consecrated' the country by lighting a beacon at the mouth of every stream.

Nothing more is known about the lands of the 'ryger' until the Battle of *Hafrsfjord* (872—or possibly some twenty-five years later, according to some modern historians). After *Harald Fairhair* had won all Trøndelag and Vestlandet in a succession of victories during a period of seven years, he advanced south along the coast to challenge an alliance of 'kings' from Hordaland, Rogaland, Agder and Telemark. Another source—which appears more reliable—states that he had to contend with only two kings, 'Kjotve the Wealthy of Kvinne (Kvina) and Utstein' (a king in Agder) and 'Haklang.' It seems certain that contingents came across from Ireland and the Scottish Isles to oppose the encroachments of Harald Fairhair upon their lands of origin, and that among them was *Olav the White* of Dublin. Historians are at variance as to whether the latter king was one and the same as 'Haklang'—who was killed in the battle, whereas Kjotve fled. The saga writer—Torbjørn Hornklove—gives a vivid description of the bloody battle afloat and of the hectic flight across the plain of Jæren. To emphasize the completeness of the victory he states that Harald took over 'Kvinne and Utstein which were 'kongsgaarder' in foreign lands, i.e. in the Kingdom of Sørlandet.

Kjotve had fought to keep the invader out of his domains, but Harald strengthened his control of the entire west coast by making his 'kongsgaard' at *Avaldsnes* the royal dwelling, whence he could control the passage of all shipping through the narrow channel of Karmsound at his feet. It was a key position controlling all coastal communications. Harald found that Rogaland and Sørlandet were governed by ancient custom through a number of petty chiefs and 'haulds'—a series of local communities linked loosely together.

When Harald grew old, he decreed at a 'ting' on Lake Mjøsa

a division of his kingdom among his sons whilst he himself retained midtlandet, i.e. the fylker which held their 'ting' at Gulen on Sognefjord. Both Rogaland and Agder attended Gulating at that period. *Harald Fairhair* died at Avaldsnes (*ca.* 933), and was buried on Karmsound, where Snorre saw his reputed burial place three hundred years after his committal. He gave a vivid description of the spot, but modern archæologists are able to demonstrate that the 'tomb' he saw was too old by centuries. At *Gar*, *ca.* 2 km. north of Haugesund and on the mainland, 'Haralds Monument' was erected on what was considered the thousandth anniversary of his victory at Hafrsfjord (1872) and of the unification of the realm of Norway. On the shore hard-by and close to the barrow, stands a venerable stone cross from the earliest Christian period.

An outstanding ship-grave at Storhaug—on Karmøy just north of Avaldsnes—was excavated in 1886, and about 3 km. south of it is Grønnhaug (excavated 1902). They are on the spot where Harald Fairhair had his 'kongsgaard'; alas, only slender remains of the Storhaug boat survive. There was also a 'cenotaph' grave called 'Salhushaugen' on Karmøy (excavated 1907), which was shown conclusively to contain no burial although it was a considerable barrow measuring no less than 40 yards in diameter. It must have been raised to commemorate members of the royal family who died overseas or were drowned.

The forces of the 'sons of Gunhild' met those of Haakon I (the Good) at Reheia—the 'tingplace' at Avaldsnes. There Haakon killed his nephew Guttorm, and the latter's brothers fled back to Denmark after suffering great losses.

Following the Battle of Fitjar (961) Norway was divided up among the victors. Rogaland came under Haakon Jarl the Mighty —he acting as 'earl' for King Harald Bluetooth of Denmark. The latter also controlled Agder and Viken through Bjørn Farmann of Skiringsal (a son of Harald Fairhair), and later through Harald Grenske.

Each fylke had its sacrificial centre in heathen times, that for *Ryfylke* (Ryggjafylki) being at Lygi (now Lye). The 'kongsgaard' at Avaldsnes (*ca.* 10 km. south of Haugesund) was undoubtedly an important religious centre: it later became the site of a thirteenth century church which is still the fourth largest rural church in all Norway. Its silhouette on a promontory is a fine sight as one passes through Karmsound.

Erik the Red and Greenland

Erik Raude of Rogaland, a crude but able man of great determination, was not the actual discoverer of Greenland but the first to operate there. At the age of twenty he had to flee Norway after committing a murder, and sailed to Iceland. He married and cleared some ground in Haukadal, but having soon afterwards committed another series of murders he was outlawed for three years. He fitted out a vessel to seek a country which had been sighted earlier, and set foot ashore at a spot called Blaaserk. Erik spent three winters on Greenland, and explored its coast from Cape Farewell at its southernmost tip, all along Davis Strait and into the deep fjords. That voyage of Erik Raude was one of the most noteworthy of ancient times.

When he returned to Iceland he named his promised land 'Greenland,' in the hope that that attractive title would appeal to possible immigrants. That same summer (984) twenty-five ships set sail, but no more than fourteen fetched up, and the colony was established, over which he ruled as 'lord' and his family took the lead in the new community. He himself was anti-Christian, but his wife received baptism, and when his son *Leiv Eriksson* was in Trondheim he too adopted the new Faith at the hands of Olav Tryggvesson. Leiv Eriksson was leader of the mission to convert Greenland, and thence he made his epoch-making voyage to discover America and, having run down its coast as far as Chesapeake Bay, he called the new country 'Vinland.'

Olav (I) Tryggvesson

After Olav I had baptised all Viken, he carried the Cross into Agder. Having made many concessions to the people of Rogaland, they too accepted baptism, and Olav married his own sister off to its great chieftain, *Erling Skjalgsson of Sola*, head of the most influential family in all Vestlandet. Owing to his mediation

Olav was in close touch with all the Vestland chiefs, though he himself lived mostly in Trøndelag during his short reign.

Olav, as is well known, perished at Svolder (1000), and in the division of the spoils among the victors, the earls Erik and Svein were allotted all the country between Haalogaland and Agder, though Erling never became their adherent and ruled more or less independently during the interregnum until 1016—just as he had during the latter years of the overlordship of Haakon Jarl, the last of the mighty heathens.

The King of the Ryger (*Ryggfskorjen*)

The most powerful opponent of Erik and Svein—who ruled all Norway on behalf of the Kings of Denmark and Sweden—was *Erling Skjalgsson of Sola*, where he maintained a small court at his 'gaard' there. He always kept a 'hird' of 90 men, but when the earls were in the vicinity his guard was increased to 245. Erling went on viking each year to collect funds to maintain his magnificence, but was a 'model employer' in his age. He permitted his slaves to work both day and night if they so desired, and named a figure at which they might purchase their freedom; this was fixed so low that any zealous worker could amass it after three years.

Erling had fought on the side of Svein as late as 1022, but later effected reconciliation with Olav II who granted him the lordship of the coast between Sognefjord and Lindesnes. Erling was so generally feared that all gave him implicit obedience, and at length Olav sensed he was wielding too much power. The latter then appointed his good friend *Aslak Fitjaskalle*—who was also a relative of Erling—as his agent in Sunnhordland, with instructions to keep Erling in his place. This division of authority was not at all to Erling's taste, and very soon Aslak had to lay complaint against him to Olav who summoned Erling to Tønsberg. The differences of opinion were somehow smoothed out, and all apparently became good friends once again.

Asbjørn of Trondenes was a powerful thane in Troms * who wanted to maintain the usual high standard of gluttony at his seasonal feasts although corn crops had failed up north. So

* See 'North Norway.'

Asbjørn sailed down to Karmöy (1022) and asked the King's agent at his Avaldsnes 'kongsgaard' to supply him. As Olav had ordered the conservation of supplies his 'low-born' agent refused to satisfy Asbjørn and suggested he try at Sola. There, his uncle Erling told him that Olav had forbidden export and he dare not disobey him, but that his slaves might perhaps supply Asbjørn since they were outside the pale of the law. This arrangement was carried out, but on his return voyage Asbjørn foolishly stayed the night at Karmöy, where Olav's zealous 'low-born' agent had the precious cargo discharged. This 'loss of face' was too much for Asbjørn of Trondenes, so in the following spring he sneaked into Avaldsnes 'kongsgaard' where Olav was being entertained by his bailiff. Asbjørn listened through the key-hole and heard the 'low-born' agent giving the King a florid account of Asbjørn's discomfiture the previous year. In a fit of uncontrollable fury he burst into the 'hall' and cut off the head of the baseborn bailiff which fell on the table by the King's platter. The 'Easter Peace' had been broken, and word was sent to Erling that his nephew was to be executed. The condemned Asbjørn waited in chains without the church all Sunday morning whilst Olav and his men were within at Mass. At the crucial moment Erling appeared with 1,800 (?) men whom he lined up outside the church awaiting Olav's appearance. The bishop intervened and saved the life of Asbjørn who had to throw himself on Olav's mercy.

Olav had his revenge by appointing the thane Asbjørn—a nephew of the mighty Erling Skjalgsson—to succeed the 'low-born' man he had murdered in the post of royal bailiff at Avaldsnes. Asbjørn had no alternative but to accept the humiliating solution offered, but for so doing was severely upbraided by his equals among the thanes. Thenceforward no feelings of amity existed between Olav and Erling: in such wise did Olav the Saint make powerful enemies.

* * * * *

In the spring of 1027 Olav issued mobilization orders from Tønsberg, calling upon all Norwegians to join him to repel

Canute the Dane, but Viken alone complied. Olav, however, succeeded in repatriating the vessels he had abandoned at Kalmar, and in late autumn (1027) set sail for Trøndelag to assemble forces there. Canute had meanwhile appeared off the coast of Agder which caused numbers of thanes to desert Olav, including Erling Skjalgsson, to whom Canute presented the entire coast between Stadt and Rygjarbit (near Risør).

When Olav's fleet had reached the Selöyene (near Lindesnes) it was held up by contrary winds, and there he learnt that Erling had assembled many ships at Jæren. They met off Egersund a few days before Christmas, and by a ruse Olav gave Erling a false idea of his intended manœuvre. Olav worked his way into Boknfjord and ran in behind a promontory, so that when Erling entered the fjord with his solitary ship he fell into the trap. The saga gives a vivid description of the fight, and of how at length Erling stood alone on his poop refusing to plead for mercy but instead calling out: 'It is breast to breast that eagles claw one another.' Olav offered mercy, all the while snicking Erling's cheeks with his axe and taunting him. Suddenly, however, Aslak Fitjaskalle split the head of his relative Erling with his axe—when Olav cried out: 'You have struck Norway from my hand.' Sigvat Skald states that Olav and his men spent a sad Christmas after Erling's death, for all knew that it would be the signal for Egder, Ryger and Horder to combine against Olav—who had then of necessity to flee Norway and to make his way to Russia.

Rogaland in the Eleventh Century

With the death of the great *Erling Skjalgsson* (1027) followed the rapid eclipse of Sola as Vestlandets political centre, and by the end of the century its former glories had faded away.

Rogaland took no distinctive part in the struggle between St. Olav and Canute the Great, nor does it appear to have been embroiled in the exciting events during the reign of Harald Haardraade. No doubt it supplied several units to the fleet which sailed away from Herdla with his invading force, and several 'rogalendinger' surely bit the dust with their king when he was killed at the Battle of Stamford Bridge, near York (1066).

Olav III (Kyrre) returned from that abortive invasion bringing several fugitive English thanes to Norway, and very possibly it was their influence that induced 'Olav the Peaceful' to introduce reforms into his country—e.g. guilds—and to found the town of Bergen (*ca.* 1070) as a trading centre after English models. With the birth of Bergen a drastic change took place in the means of livelihood of the people of Rogaland, and in their trading contacts with the outer world.

Whatever commodities the folk in Rogaland may have traded did not pass through any town, since none existed until Bergen was created. Erling Skjalgsson had amassed his great wealth not solely from plundering raids but also from legitimate trade—probably with the Frisians, who surely visited the snug harbour in Vaagsbotn, where Stavanger later arose. It seems safe to assume that the overseas traders came to Vaagsbotn—and perhaps Kopervik—to load the fish of North Norway as their principal cargo. What is definitely known is that they paid for much of whatever they bought there in the hard currencies of England and north-west Germany, since no fewer than four thousand coins from the first seventy years of the eleventh century have been unearthed in Rogaland. It is worth noting that all finds are dated previous to 1070—which seems to show that some royal edict arbitrarily revolutionized the channels of trade, and transferred all exchange of commodities to Olav Kyrre's royal town of Bergen. Perhaps, however, it was the new sense of security which caused people to cease burying their treasured coins.

What induced King Olav III to make this alteration in commercial practice can only be a matter for conjecture owing to the total absence of records. It is, however, obvious that the king could keep a better control of trade—and of the taxes it brought to his coffers—by forcing shipping to enter the almost landlocked harbour of Bergen. Whereas foreign-going ships could stealthily slip out of Vaagsbotn (Stavanger) into open sea, it was necessary in order to get clear of Bergen to use a passage through narrow Karmsund and past Avaldnes. Moreover, Skule Kongsfostre and Ketil Krok—the two former English thanes to whose advice King Olav would have listened—had considerable interests in the fish trade of North Norway, and would have wished to market their produce at a port where security was assured against raiders or evasionists.

Whatever may have been King Olav's purpose in pauperizing the harbours of Rogaland to establish Bergen, the fact remains that Rogaland went into a decline after 1070.

* * * * *

It is generally supposed that *Gulating*—the 'parliament' of Western Norway—was established (*ca.* 940) by Haakon I (the Good) on the advice of 'Thorleiv the Wise,' who was a paternal uncle of Erling Skjalgsson of Sola. Elleka-skald makes it clear that Rogaland was subject to Gulating as early as 986.

In the version of Gulating Law ascribed to Olav the Saint (*ca.* 1020) it is laid down that 102 representatives from Hordaland, the same number from Rogaland, and 29 from Agder, are bound to attend its meetings. It is known that in the twelfth century 'Gulatingslagen' extended to Rygjarbit—just east of Risør—which was the eastern limit of the lands of the 'ryger' in ancient tribal times.

The Universal Law of Magnus V (1274) altered the geographical limits of Gulating jurisdiction but reduced representation to: Rogaland 30, Hallingdal 4, Otrada 14, and Setesdal 2.

In those far-off days disputes were first taken before the equivalent of Petty Sessions, then to the fylketing (High Court) and finally before the Gulating (acting as Supreme Court).

Today Rogaland is still within the jurisdiction of Gulating, whose Criminal Court Sessions (Lagmannstinget) are held in Bergen—except for cases from Rogaland which are tried at Stavanger.

CHAPTER XVII

THE GREAT CLERICS: REINALD TO ARNE

The Cathedral of St. Svithun

WHEN the two kings Eystein I and Sigurd were jointly ruling Norway they frequently had disagreements, since their characters were poles apart. Eystein I continued his grandfather's support of Bergen—indeed his attractive contemporary statue was found there some time ago amid the foundations of Munkeliv Abbey. On Eystein's death (1122) his brother 'Sigurd the Crusader,' perhaps from motives of jealousy, reversed Eystein's policy and split the diocese of Gulating in two by building a cathedral at Stavanger (*ca.* 1125).

King Sigurd appointed as its first bishop, Reinald, an Englishman, who whilst studying at Winchester would have been present when its cathedral was dedicated (1093) to Saint Svithun. What more natural than that Reinald should dedicate his new cathedral to the same saint, whose day in Norway was altered from 15th July to 2nd July, i.e. the day on which he died at Winchester when its bishop in A.D. 860. The 'Eve of St. Svithunsmessa'—1st July—was *syftesok*, having been so called in both Gulating and Frostating Laws. 'Syfte' denoted 'to clean,' and tradition ordained that two brooms be set up crosswise in every field on that day to sweep them clear of tares and weeds.

St. Svithun was the saint of the *weather* just as in England, but he was never especially cultivated in Norway, being regarded as a foreign importation with no background in folklore. The term 'St. Svithun's town' was used for Stavanger throughout the Middle Ages, and a shrine in the cathedral contained part of an arm of the saint which was last catalogued in 1517.

Bishop Reinald's church survives in much of the nave and West Tower, but the chancel is of thirteenth century construction. The restoration of 1869 revealed the inadequacy of its foundations, even as those of Winchester were recently discovered to be dangerously meagre. Yet both magnificent fanes have survived through more than eight centuries. English and French models are manifest in doorways and pillar-capitals—indeed one of the latter is a twin of one in Canterbury cathedral—though no two are alike; it seems certain they were carved by English masons.

The cathedral, which was completed *ca.* 1150, is one of the oldest stone churches in Norway—earlier than Trondheim, Hamar or St. Magnus in Kirkwall, Orkneys—though in comparison with any of them it is but a small building. Two stone churches of similar date survive at Talgje and Sørbø, and there are also several very early fonts in Rogaland, but nothing remains of Reinald's church furnishings.

The present 'kongsgaard' was begun by Reinald for his bishop's palace, and remnants of Norman work remain in its cellars and foundations.

Very little is known concerning Bishop Reinald himself, but he surely studied architecture at Winchester—as was the custom with many priests in his age. Some years after King Sigurd had returned from the Crusades he introduced payment of *tithe* to the Church, and Reinald worked out the details for his diocese. This tax did not by any means suffice to meet the demands of Reinald for his building operations, so it was a fortunate chance that brought Sigurd into matrimonial difficulties. The King had wearied of his Queen Malmfrid and, like our own Henry VIII, wanted to be rid of her and marry a Lady Cecilia. He applied first to Bishop Magne of Bergen, who would not contemplate for one moment permitting the commission of such a breach of Canon Law, despite threats of violence uttered by the angry monarch. So Sigurd turned to Reinald, who offered similar objections which, however, were overcome when the King tempted him with a vast sum for the erection of his beloved cathedral. According to Snorre this mercenary deal was effected in A.D. 1128: it profited Sigurd little, since he died two years later.

12. Lindesnes, the southernmost point of Norway

Idyllic Gamle Hellesund

13. Rygnestadloftet, medieval house, Setesdal

Valle, Setesdal

The Civil War (1130–1240)

'The Century of the Pretenders' began with the death of Sigurd, and threw all Norway into the turmoil of Civil War—actually a clash between East and West Norway. Bishop Reinald made it obvious that he supported Magnus III (the Blind), and so fell foul of Harald Gille when he usurped the throne (1135). That Irish cut-throat hanged Bishop Reinald at Bergen because he would or could not divulge the hiding place of Magnus' treasure. Reinald was buried in St. Michael's church, Nordnes (Bergen) on 18th January, 1135, and his successor was Jon Birgersson (probably King Harald's nominee), who was later consecrated as first archbishop of Trondheim by Cardinal Nicholas Breakespeare in 1153. It seems probable that the cardinal selected him because Rogaland occupied a somewhat neutral position between East and West Norway, i.e. between the three joint kings. It was Cardinal Nicholas who granted Stavanger a cathedral chapter, which at a later date was to violently dispute the authority of its bishop.

After the death of the last of the *joint* kings, Eystein II (1157), hostility between the two parties to the Civil War became acute. Erling Skakke of Sunnhordland was Vestlandet's leader, and succeeded in securing the coronation of his son, Magnus IV, at Bergen in 1164. As a coronation gift the young king presented the town of Stavanger to the bishopric of St. Svithun—no doubt with a view to securing Rogaland for his cause. Stavanger as a '*Bishop's town*' was thus placed in an unique position: it was a wise move on Erling's part to thus secure the bishop's support at a critical juncture in his family affairs. Aamund was bishop at the time, but he resigned in 1171 to become Abbot of Olav's abbey in Stavanger—a post he occupied for twelve years.

Nothing is known of the existence of this Olav's abbey before 1204, except for a reference to 'The Abbey in Stavanger' (*ca.* 1160) by Reginald of Durham in his 'Life of St. Cuthbert.' He wrote that a thane, Thorolv of Sola, was a powerful prelate of high birth and much wealth. He entered his son in Stavanger abbey for higher education, and after five years there he came under the care of a new and very learned teacher. Drinking and dissipation brought on 'St. Vitus Dance' and other paralytic afflictions which placed him beyond the pale for many years. His distressed father handed him over to a brother—also a priest —who took him on pilgrimages to many a holy shrine. After six years thus spent without improvement he came to Durham in 1172, where his complete recovery took place to the joy and wonder of all. Reginald of Durham wrote that he was told this story by the young Norwegian himself.

Erik, a remarkable man, succeeded to the bishopric in 1171. He had studied at St. Victor's, Paris (1150), and later rose to be Archbishop of Trondheim. He was Sverre's most implacable enemy when that usurper seized power (1178), and a leader of the Vestland party during the struggle for the mastery of Bergen which became the crux of the whole Civil War. In Rogaland there were several noble families who fervently espoused the cause of Erling Skakke and Magnus IV throughout the most critical period of the Civil War, although Rogaland itself was never a battlefield during its final stages.

After Magnus' defeat at Nordnes, Bergen (1181), he fled to Stavanger, where Bishop Erik persuaded him to rally his forces and return to Bergen to take Sverre by surprise. That element failed, however, for Sverre escaped to Trondheim, whence he returned in the following year to assert his superiority so far as to appoint his own sysselmann in Rogaland to collect taxes and maintain his cause. He revoked the gift of Magnus IV to St. Svithun, and Bishop Erik was powerless to oppose him.

When the famous Archbishop Eystein Erlendsen died (1188) it was claimed that he had nominated Erik of Stavanger as his successor. Sverre naturally raised objections to the advancement of such a prominent opponent, but nevertheless deemed it expedient to acquiesce. After much dispute between Sverre, the new archbishop, and Stavanger chapter as to who should fill *its* vacant throne, the choice fell on *Njaal* (probably Nigel—an Englishman or Scot) who was consecrated in Stavanger (1190). Four years later he was reluctantly compelled to assist three fellow bishops at the coronation of Sverre in Bergen (1194)— an event which brought the King into violent conflict with the

Church since the Pope had already excommunicated him. The four Norwegian bishops who had crowned the banned monarch were themselves put under the ban by the Pope himself, in the presence of a large gathering in St. Peters, Rome, on 18th November, 1194.

Times were difficult for Bishop Njaal: Archbishop Erik wrote to the Pope about 'the godless and lying bishops,' and at length Njaal succeeded in reconciling himself with Erik and the great Danish Archbishop Absalon—indeed so completely that at his death (1201) the latter left Njaal a legacy.

Sverre died at Bergen in March 1202, and then Njaal returned to his bishopric after an exile of five years. Stavanger Diocese at that time embraced Rogaland, Agder, Valdres and Hallingdal. Cardinal Nicholas Breakespeare (1153) had granted Stavanger the parish of Eidfjord—an enclave at the head of Inner Hardangerfjord—to permit the bishop to proceed to the distant valleys of Valdres and Hallingdal without leaving his own diocese. Eidfjord remained with Stavanger until 1601, and the two valleys were not separated from it until 1631.

In the cleaning-up operations following Sverre's death, Haakon III sent a strong fleet south from Trondheim to oppose the 'bagler' squadron he knew to be sailing round the coast from Oslo. The 'birchlegs'—led by Peter Steyper and Einar Kongsmaag (who had married Cecilia, Sverre's daughter)—arrived one evening at Rott, off Jæren, and learnt that the 'bagler' were in Stavanger. The latter in ignorance of their danger, rowed out next morning into Boknfjord where they were routed utterly. From that moment Rogaland, led by Bishop Njaal, ceased all hostility towards Sverre's family and successors.

In the spring of 1205 Einar Kongsmaag, then sysselmann of Rogaland, was surprised by a force of 'bagler' and took refuge up the tower of St. Svithun's. When the 'bagler' caught him they extracted an oath on the shrine of St. Svithun that he would never take up arms against their king, Erling Steinvegg. However, no sooner was he outside the cathedral than they killed Einar and fifty of his followers: then they systematically plundered Stavanger. It is a tradition that the stone cross now in the garden of Stavanger's museum—one of the finest from the Middle Ages—is connected with that murder. The runic inscription indicates there was a town here at the time.

Peter Steyper then took over the syssel, but was also surprised by King Philip's 'bagler.' He succeeded in escaping and continued to serve the 'birchlegs' in Rogaland. After the Treaty on Kvitesøy (1208) he found life too dull, and went on crusade with his wife, and that great adventurer Reidar Sendemann—whence he never returned.

It is significant that Bishop Nicholas Arnesson of Oslo should have chosen a spot in Rogaland to convene a meeting of 'bagler' and 'birchlegs' to compose their differences. It seems to show that Rogaland was considered to be in some measure *neutral* between the two major parties to the Civil War. Around a table on the outlying island of Kvitesøy an armistice was concluded which enabled all Norway to enjoy some years of comparative peace.

Bishop Njaal died in 1207 after a turbulent period of seventeen years on his throne. He must have gained deep respect since parents in Rogaland have given their boys his name for centuries; even today the form 'Njædell' is quite common in the fylke.

Yet a third Englishman succeeded him as bishop—Henrik (1207–24)—but little is known of his rule since they were peaceful years. He met King Haakon IV at Egersund (1219) when, following Henrik's acute hostility to the choice of that monarch, the two were reconciled. There was little resultant effect since Stavanger and Rogaland no longer played an important role in Norwegian political life. Henrik's brass seal-die was found near Ribe some years ago, and is now in Oslo Historical Museum. It is the oldest Norwegian matrix known.

The first 'lagmann' (man-of-law) to be mentioned in Ryfylke was in 1224—he supported Skule against King Haakon IV.

Henrik's successor was King Haakon's chaplain, Askell Jonssøn, who was sent on an embassy to Henry III in 1225. During the troubles between the King and Skule the bishop wisely kept himself and his diocese outside the disputes.

In the closing years of the Civil War Rogaland was with

King Haakon, despite the fact that the sysselmann—Baard of Hestby (Hesby), the first of that great family to appear in history—had been an adherent of Skule. He vacated his syssel, however, when Skule began open hostilities against the King, and swore fealty to Haakon. No major event occurred in Rogaland during those last troubled years of Civil War which ended with Skule's death (1240).

Years of Peace and Plenty

King Haakon IV showed his gratitude to Rogaland by staying a while in Stavanger during 1243—the first King of Norway ever so to do. It appears that Bishop Askell persuaded him to renew Magnus IV's gift of the town to St. Svithun; the decree of renewal is engrossed on the most ancient and important parchment concerning Stavanger that survives. By it all Crown Lands were transferred to the See. The effect of this unique position caused loss of interest in Stavanger among the kings of later times, and this hampered its development. Nevertheless 1243 ushered in a golden era for its ecclesiastical life. After he had crowned Haakon IV (1247) in Bergen, Cardinal William of Sabina (Modena) spent some days in Stavanger.

It was surely during Askell's time (*ca.* 1250) that the Augustinian Abbey on the island of *Utstein*—dedicated to St. Laurence—was founded: its ruins today are the most complete of any Norwegian abbey. It seems certain that it absorbed 'Olav's kloster' in Stavanger, which stood on the site now occupied by the Kielland family mausoleum. The stone churches at Ogna and Orre—now so mutilated—and also the ruins of Sola church, bear witness to the handiwork of Bishop Askell (died 1254).

'Crown Prince' *Magnus* (later V) was granted Ryfylke in fief, and took up residence in Stavanger for a few years. After his wedding at Bergen (1261) to Princess Ingeborg of Denmark—and their coronation—they spent three months honeymoon at Stavanger. Two years later he recruited troops in Rogaland for the Scottish campaign, and then proceeded to Bergen to act as 'regent' while his father was across the North Sea. King Haakon had taken Bishop Thorgils of Stavanger on his expedition; to whom it fell to wash the King's body and shave him after his death at Kirkwall in the Orkneys (1263).

On the accession of Magnus he sent an Englishman, Canan Adam of Stavanger, to London to announce the demise of Haakon IV. Adam returned with a missive expressing regret at the passing of the great King. Magnus, a disciple of the gentle St. Francis, founded many hospitals: it was at his prompting that Bishop Thorgils established one at Stavanger—probably for lepers.

Then in 1272 that town was swept by a disastrous fire, which devastated the cathedral and destroyed the shrine of St. Svithun. Work on restoration of the nave and an enlarged chancel was at once put in hand, and to obtain the necessary funds the archbishop issued in November 1275—for the very first time in Norway—a *letter of dispensation* for all sins committed by subscribers.

Bishop Thorgils died (1276), and with the erection of the new Gothic chancel and the 'dispensations' a new chapter of Stavanger history opens.

Arne—The Fighting Bishop (1276–1303)

This remarkable man occupied the throne of the See of Stavanger for twenty-six years under extremely difficult conditions. His obsession was the erection of a superb Gothic chancel, and in order to raise funds for that purpose he stooped to any wile to obtain 'dispensations' from numerous Scandinavian bishops. The Pope himself was induced by Arne to grant one in 1290, and Arne's drive was so forceful that his cathedral was completed before his death in 1303.

The 'Early English' architecture of both the Gothic chancel and Bishop's private chapel survive as memorials of Arne's zeal—the twenty-five sculptured heads with which he adorned them being of especial interest, since they are portraits of his contemporaries. The finest of them is that of Arne himself wearing his mitre, whilst three of the others represent King Magnus V, and his two sons Erik II and Haakon V. The last-named king probably had much to say regarding the middle stages of reconstruction, since not only did he hold Ryfylke in fief as 'Duke' before he ascended the throne—and lived there much during the lifetime of his brother—but he also retained as his hird-priest one Galfrid, an Englishman, who quite likely exercised a considerable influence on the reconstruction plans.

'Duke' Haakon later had as chancellor Aake, a remarkable man who, after 1292, played a leading part in Stavanger during Arne's violent disputes with his cathedral chapter. The bishop wanted to deprive the chapter of some of their perquisites in order to swell his 'Restoration Fund,' but the chapter took another view. Even after King Haakon had taken the side of the chapter the bishop refused to abandon his predatory schemes, and appealed to the Pope. A committee appointed by the highest ecclesiastical authority gave judgment for the chapter, but even then Arne refused to submit and so, with great reluctance on both sides, this quarrel between two Church authorities was referred to the highest secular power—King Haakon—since the clerics were busy excommunicating each other and made no progress towards a settlement. The royal decision went against Arne, whereupon the chapter exulted defiantly. Yet disputes continued between them until the turbulent bishop died (1303). His chancel and beautiful house chapel (known today as 'Munkekirken') have left his name and memory towering above all dissension and dispute.

* * * * *

During the minority of the two sons of Magnus V in the 1280's, a number of anti-clerical thanes acquired great power. *Baron* Gaut of Tolga, who owned the large estate of Talgøy in Ryfylke, was one of these, and was the first of his family to be ennobled. He met an accidental death during a drinking bout in Stavanger (1288), and his inebriated assailant sought sanctuary in St. Svithun: he was, however, dragged out by *Isak Gautssøn* and murdered. Isak, who had been a member of the Embassy to arrange the marriage of Princess Margaret (1287), harboured Count Jakob of Halland—one of the murderers of King Erik Glipping of Denmark. Count Jakob's daughter married Isak, and they produced a daughter whose tombstone at Fjære (Grimstad) was erroneously attributed by some antiquaries in 1814 to the infant daughter of that Princess de Joigny whom Audun Hugleikssøn was accused of seducing.* Isak had ships in England at the time of his death (1303).

There was little or no trade, shipping or fish export from Stavanger—factors which caused other Norwegian towns to progress during the thirteenth century. Stavanger was exclusively an ecclesiastical town, and the clerics formed the basis of its existence.

* See 'West Norway and its Fjords.'

CHAPTER XVIII

ARNE TO HOSKOLDSSON

The Fourteenth Century

THERE were many who breathed more freely when the pugnacious Bishop Arne went to his rest (1303), and was succeeded by Ketill—a man of peace and moderation, who played an important role also in national affairs until his death (1317).

After Duke Haakon had become king (1299) he no longer found time to spare for Rogaland—busy as he was countering the intrigues of the *Hansa* who, however, had no ambitions concerning the port of Stavanger. When King Haakon V had to select an ambassador to send to Edward II his choice was Canon Hugo of Stavanger, an Englishman, who negotiated a renewal of the Treaty concluded between Henry III and Magnus V.

King Haakon obtained from Bishop Ketill in 1305, the advowson of St. Olav's church at *Avaldsnes*, which then became one of the fourteen royal chapels: three of the remainder were in Stavanger Diocese, viz.: Sørbø on Rennesøy, Huseby in Lister, and Egersund. The independent position of these royal chapels from control by the Church hierarchy was to cause many troubles in later years.

King Haakon established a special 'lagting' at Avaldsnes, to which the folk of Rogaland and Agder might bring their pleas and obtain redress, and thus be spared the long journey to Bergen or Gulen to attend Gulating. Throughout his life Haakon V had been a benefactor to Rogaland, and at death bequeathed many treasures to Avaldsnes church, including 'a bell cast in England by Siglavus.' His testament confirmed all the privileges granted to Avaldsnes by himself and his Queen Euphemia.

* * * * *

Troubles rained upon Norway following the death of Haakon V (1319), due in part to the frivolity of his daughter, the Duchess Ingeborg, but also to the union of the Crown with Sweden in the person of his three-year-old grandson. During this period of uncertainty the family of *Hestby* from Finnøy came to play a leading part in national history, in the persons of *Finn and Ivar Ogmundssøn.* Those two brothers were among the 'Twelve-man Council' of the Kingdom (1319), and during the thirty years of misrule by Magnus VI, those two 'rogalendinger' were frequently in opposition to the great Erling Vidkunnssøn. Scandal told that Ivar Ogmundssøn was far too fond of the Duchess Ingeborg (mother of Magnus VI), and their intimacy led to a violent quarrel (1329) with that flighty princess's second husband, Knut Porse, two years after their marriage.

Ivar was appointed 'drott' (viceroy) by Magnus in 1334, and five years later the two brothers were the most powerful men in the country—to whose advice the King was obliged to listen respectfully.

Quarrel between Bishop and Abbot

The Ogmundssøn most closely connected with Stavanger was *Erik*, who occupied its bishop's throne for twenty years (1322–42). His dispute with Abbot Erik of *Utstein* was a *cause célèbre* in their generation, since luscious scandal in a monastery gave everybody a delectable subject for gossip.

The two high prelates were diametrically opposite in character, the bishop peace-loving and cultured, the abbot crude and brutal. The latter administered the lands of the abbey indifferently, whilst his treatment of his monks was harsh and inconsiderate. At length Bishop Erik felt compelled to step in, and in the autumn of 1333 paid a visit to the island monastery and found the doors barred and bolted. Thereupon he forced an entry and sang Mass in the abbey church, summoned Abbot Erik to Stavanger and suspended him from office.

The Abbot laid his case before the archbishop, and this compelled the bishop to substantiate *his* case. The charge read: 'that Abbot Erik had for several years, in contravention of the Rules of the Order, spent nights in dissipation with a young lady of high degree—that he had taught her a language none could understand and in which they conversed. Moreover, he had cultivated the fields belonging to the lady at the expense of the abbey—that this female had been permitted to sing in the Brethren's refectory. . . . That it was a notorious fact that the abbot had earlier murdered a young girl . . .' and the bishop continued with details of a series of iniquities and misdemeanours.

The bishop's charges were passed on to the Pope (1334), because the abbot had appealed to the Holy Father in Avignon. There it would appear that the abbot had oiled palms out of the riches of his monastery lands, for although the final judgment is not known it appears that Bishop Erik did not come too well out of the affair. Yet it speaks well for the bishop that he was a trusted friend of Bishop Haakon of Bergen, who was one of the most respected men of his day.

Nothing is known concerning Stavanger during the first troublous thirty years of the reign of Magnus VI, which closed with the scourge of the Black Death (1349). That devastated Stavanger, and its ecclesiastical set-up was struck a blow from which it never recovered. As the Church was the town's *raison d'être*, its consequences are obvious. Its bishop, Guttorm, and Ivar Ogmundssøn both died of the pest, but the latter's nephew, *Ogmund Finnssøn*, survived to champion Norway through many difficult decades.

All Norway in the Doldrums

Hardly had the worst ravages of the Black Death passed before King Magnus and his young son Haakon paid a visit to Stavanger, though there was little to be done to set the town on its feet again. To make matters even worse, Pope Clement VI in Avignon arbitrarily appointed a Swede as its bishop, and later sent a hypocritical letter to King Magnus stating that he had transferred that bishop to Oslo. Avignon's interference deprived Rogaland Diocese of a responsible leader at a critical moment, and five years were to pass before a bishop of Norwegian birth was enthroned. All that time the Pope was extracting his pound of flesh out of the assets of Rogaland's church: agriculture in

Jæren and Ryfylke had been paralysed by the effects of the Plague and the years were lean ones—but the Pope demanded his dues all the same.

The Hansa launched forth aggressively during Norway's twilight, and Bergen suffered under the encroachments of the Lübeckers who, however, sailed past Stavanger since it had no trade to attract them. Early in 1367 the viceroy, Ogmund Finnssøn, retaliated, and, after committing several acts of piracy, seized a Lübeck ship at Egersund. Then hostilities broke out openly, and the Dutch Hansa cities took a violent revenge. Their intentions were discovered by Ogmund when he captured a a vessel near Stavanger in January 1368, and shortly afterwards a Dutch squadron arrived off Lindesnes and ravaged fifteen parishes in Agder before continuing their raids on the coasts of the Kattegat.

After thus striking terror the Hansa thought fit to negotiate, and sent an embassy to Ogmund Finnssøn during the autumn of 1368. The two parties met at Avaldsnes, but when agreement failed some German ships appeared, and ravaged the west coast, especially Jæren and Ryfylke. They burnt the 'kongsgaard' at Avaldsnes and numerous dwellings in Karmsund, Ryfylke and Sogndal—as well as Bergen. In the following year King Haakon VI concluded a truce, and twelve months later Valdemar of Denmark signed the disastrous Treaty of Stralsund (1370).

When King Haakon VI died in 1380, Ogmund Finnssøn of Hestby was again appointed 'drott' (viceroy), a post which he held till his death in Halsnøy abbey, Sunnhordland, in 1388. He was the last national figure who was a native of the fylke, and left all his property 'between Stavanger and Aaen Sira (Åna Sira)' to Stavanger chapter in order that masses might be said for his soul. Ogmund was to have visited England in 1384, and Richard II provided him with a 'safe conduct'—but for some reason unknown the journey was never undertaken.

After the Kalmar Union

Queen Margaret the Great busied herself filling vacant bishops' thrones with her own nominees, who were frequently Danes or

Swedes, but how old Haakon Ivarssøn got his appointment to Stavanger in 1400 is not known. He was at that time elderly, and by 1417 quite unable to perambulate his diocese, so that Rogaland was again without an efficient governor. In 1424 he must have been quite senile, since the chapter petitioned Pope Martin 'that he had been impossible for the past three years—that he was unable to move and his physical presence so offensive that nobody would enter it.'

At last *Audun* Eyvindssøn was consecrated by three Swedish bishops in the abbey church of Vadstena (1426)—a man who, like Arne his predecessor more than a century earlier, was to earn a prominent name in the history of Rogaland in the Middle Ages. It was in the previous year (1425) that King Erik of Pommern granted a 'town charter' to Stavanger—and thus with evidence of royal interest and a strong bishop on its throne, there was every possibility for a period of progress for the fylke. A trading community began to establish itself, and to replace clerics as the progressive element in Stavanger. Germans began, for the first time, to infiltrate into its priesthood and amongst its citizens—no doubt King Erik had some responsibility for this, and a new era began which endured until 1600.

A factor in the life of Rogaland and Agder at this period was its sysselmann, *Eindrid Erlendsson*, a member of the powerful Losna family—who resided at Tønsberghus. A friend of Bishop Audun as also of most of Norway's influential men, he was employed by King Erik as Ambassador to Scotland (1429), and shortly after that journey Audun and Eindrid were captured by English pirates and submitted to many indignities. Their rough handling was the subject of representations by King Erik to Henry VI's attorneys, who gave them considerable sums in compensation.

Audun faithfully supported Erik of Pommern in his struggles with the Hansa, with the Swedes in rebellion under Engelbrekt Engelbrektsson, and he was the mediator in Amund Bolt's Norwegian rebellion (1436). When the Norwegian Committee which had been assigned the task of pleading with King Erik to return from Gotland, was waylaid by the Danes, it sent a desperate plea to Audun to come to Lødøse and assist 'for King Erik's sake as well as our own.'

It would seem that Audun did not attend the meeting of the State Council which paved the way for Christoffer of Bayern to assume the Crown of Norway—confirmed at Lødøse in 1442. Audun must, however, share responsibility for founding the Dano-Norwegian Union, since he acquiesced in it by obtaining as a *quid pro quo* confirmation of all former privileges granted to St. Svithun.

That Audun was a man of action was shown when his treasurer was captured in the dead of night off Stavanger. Audun hurriedly manned his boats, overtook the criminals and had them all hanged 'in the name of Christ.' Peder Clausson wrote (*ca.* 1600) that he 'made great improvements in churches throughout the diocese.' After nineteen years of outstanding benefit to Stavanger, he died in November 1445.

* * * * *

Then burst upon the scene a remarkable man, *Olav Nilssøn*, a Dane to whom Erik of Pommern granted Ogmund Finssøn's former estates of Hestby and Tolga. Those two men had a great affinity in their delight in piracy, and Olav was the scourge of the narrow seas until made Governor of Bergenhus. He worked for the election of the Swedish king, Karl VIII Knutssøn, to the throne of Norway: nobody else from Rogaland took part in the disputes between Swedish Karl and Danish Christian. After his accession, King Christian I paid a visit to Stavanger and took away a copy of Haakon IV's gift to St. Svithun, in order to include it in his 'capitulation.' The royal secretary, however, committed amazing errors in his transcription by attributing the original to Haakon V and Bishop Audun—but all was righted and Stavanger received yet another confirmation of the background of its ecclesiastical privileges.

Olav's exciting life story belongs to the history of Bergen* where he was murdered by the Germans in 1455—one of the most notorious crimes in Norwegian history.

After the murder the Germans hurried to Stavanger and broke

* 'See West Norway and its Fjords.'

open the cathedral sacristy to abstract all gold and silver from the treasure chests of Olav and his wife Elitza (Elizabeth)—who was, like her husband, a Dane. Thence they went to Talgøy (Tolga) to plunder and devastate. Olav's children and servants fled, and years afterwards Axel Nilssøn wrote: 'I was three years old when we escaped to the woods where we were reduced to drinking the juice of sour apples; we hid for six weeks until Mortensdag (10th November).'

King Christian I was probably glad to be quit of his Governor of Bergen, and took no action to avenge Olav Nilssøn. So it was left to the widow and her sons to harass the Hansa by piracy through a number of years. Many legends concerning Olav live on in folk-memory around Talgøy.

In 1463 Alv Thorgaardssøn began his reign as bishop which lasted eighteen years, for which no records are available. Then came Eiliv Jonsson (1481) whose thirty-one years on the throne are equally devoid of references. Throughout all the half-century covered by those two bishops life at Stavanger stagnated more and more: times were very bad. Yet the town was fortunate to have been almost by-passed by the Hansa, who were lording it over Bergen during those years.

The Reformation

The last of the twenty-eight Roman Catholic bishops of Stavanger, *Hoskold Hoskoldssøn*, acceeded in 1513: he played a feeble role throughout a desperate crisis. At a National Assembly in Copenhagen in the summer of 1515 (called to acclaim Christian II king) judges were appointed to examine a scandalous dispute between Bishop Hoskold and Abbot Henrik of *Utstein* (surely a foreigner). The latter accused the bishop of breaking into the abbey (1514) with an armed force—a drastic action not to be expected from him judging by his later falterings. The origin of the dispute was that some French and Scottish emissaries were wrecked somewhere in Ryfylke, and when they sought refuge in Stavanger the bishop refused assistance. The abbot felt his own responsibility and accompanied the ambassadors to Copenhagen. In his absence Hoskold sent a party to Utstein to seize provisions and other stores, but reconciliation after this high-handed action was brought about through the mediation of the Archbishop of Trondheim.

Yet twice during the spring of 1515 the bishop used force to break his way into the abbey, laid the monastery under the ban, and imprisoned the abbot for one hundred days in a wretched cell in Stavanger—but 'God, the Virgin Mary and St. Anne helped me to escape.' The above account is that of Abbot Henrik since Bishop Hoskold's version of events has not survived. The outcome of the dispute is not known, but later events showed that the bishop was anxious to preserve the independence of the abbey against the attempts of adherents of the Danish party to take possession of Utstein.

The chief cause of unrest in Rogaland during the reign of Christian II was the heavy taxation imposed to pay for the long war against Sweden, which closed with the notorious 'Stockholm Blood-bath' (1520). His ruthless Governor of Bergen, *Jørgen Hanssøn*, visited Ryfylke in person (1519), and meted out severe punishment to its refractory peasantry. It was on that occasion that Jon Eilivssøn (son of Stavanger's bishop) was seized and executed at Bergen.

Bishop Hoskold took the side of Frederik I, and was among those who conducted negotiations on his behalf with King Christian's Governor of Bergenhus to hand over the castle to *Vincents Lunge*. The reason the bishop championed Frederik I in early days was due to his indignation at the murder of his relative, Orm Erikssøn, by Jørgen Hanssøn. Little did Hoskold foresee, however, that he himself would be done to death in Bergen by the very men with whom he was now collaborating.

When some of Lunge's men tried to collect taxes early in 1526, they were killed by peasants from Dalane, whereupon Lunge wrote to his king that the country folk were faithful to Christian II. Then came Lunge's attempt to seize the property of Utstein abbey: he deposed the truculent Abbot Henrik and put in a bailiff of his own. Hoskold thereupon installed a new abbot, on whose sudden death Lunge tried once again to usurp but was countered by the bishop.

14. Stavanger Cathedral, exterior

Stavanger Cathedral, interior

15. Utstein Abbey

Ledaal, meeting room for the City Council

When it became clear to Hoskold that Lunge was turning 'lutheran' he, as a devout Roman Catholic, centred his hopes on a return of the exiled Christian II to the throne. The burden of the latter's heavy taxation was forgotten and the entire public in the diocese rallied to his cause, despite the fact that two of Christian's vessels cruised frequently in the waters off Rogaland Agder committing piracies during the autumn of 1525. They called at Egersund and made propaganda for a revolt, but Bishop Hoskold would have no contacts with the pirates and, at a later date, even promised to warn the new Governor of Bergen, Eske Bille, of any intelligence reports he might receive. The piracies had caused a riot in Stavanger in 1526.

As late as 1528 King Frederik I gave Bishop Hoskold and the Church of Rogaland a letter of protection, but the Lutherans were rapidly gaining ground, and in 1531 Gustav Trolle (Christian II's attorney in Norway) circulated his famous letter to all bishops—that addressed to Hoskold is the only copy that survives. In it attention was drawn to the demolition of the glorious cathedral of Bergen 'which so closely resembled Stavanger's.' Bishop Hoskold was powerless, but confidently believed that the Old Faith would triumph and placed his hopes and trust in Christian II's invasion force.

Many units of Christian's fleet were wrecked on the coasts of Lister, Jæren and Karmøy and, after arriving with the battered remnants of his Armada at Grimstad, Christian spent the winter of 1531–32 at Oslo. The rumour that Jørgen Hanssøn was on his way to Stavanger with two hundred men, proved baseless, so when on 17th February, 1532 Eske Bille and Vincents Lunge wrote Bishop Hoskold demanding his affirmation of loyalty to Frederik I, the bishop was irresolute and endeavoured to keep one foot in each camp. Unrest spread throughout the diocese, and Eske Bille began to clean up.

During the three years of 'Grevefeiden (The Count's War—1533–36) Bishop Hoskold was powerless to assist his archbishop, who played a lone hand for the independence of Norway—also as 'Defender of the Faith,' with Hoskold as his only friend among the bishops. The latter was already a sick man when he attended the Norwegian State Council held at Bud (1533).

In 1536 Eske Bille wrote to the archbishop that the entire Norwegian State Council, with the exception of Bishop Hoskold, were now prepared to elect Christian III king—and, finally, during the summer of that year Hoskold followed the lead of his colleagues. He was not man enough to hold out to the end, and that autumn he joined with Stavanger's 'lagmann' and the last Abbot of Utstein in electing the Lutheran Christian III at Bergen (1536).

Tord Rød, the new Governor of Bergen, seized the person of Hoskold Hoskoldssøn—Stavanger's last Roman Catholic bishop —and caused him to be put to death in Bergen early in 1538. This was just over four hundred years since the first Bishop of Stavanger, Reinald, had been hanged at Nordnes, Bergen. Tord Rød transferred the property of Stavanger bishopric to the Crown: its chapter was permitted to continue to exist, and played a limited role in the history of the diocese as late as the eighteenth century.

Utstein Abbey and its vast estates were granted to Trond Ivarssøn, who had formerly been bailiff to that great patriot Archbishop Olav Engelbrektssøn—but turned his coat. Trond's only liability was to provide board and lodging for the monks for so long as they might live.

CHAPTER XIX

BYWAYS OF HISTORY IN ROGALAND

The City of Stavanger

STAVANGER was in all ages a 'Bishop's town'—kings and nobles had little or no interest in it. It is one of the oldest towns in Norway—the only one in Rogaland which goes back to the Middle Ages.

At one time it possessed no fewer than five churches, of which *Maria Church* alone survived the Reformation. The last vestiges of its original construction were demolished in 1882, after a life-time of 600 years.

A school was controlled by the chapter for the training of priests, where latin, music, singing, the saints' calendar, canon law, etc., were taught. It was first mentioned in 1243, when William—surely an Englishman—was its 'magister.'

The most important duty of the bishop was the annual perambulation of his diocese. The latter was very widespread, owing to Cardinal Nicholas Breakespeare having allotted the two distant valleys of Valdres and Hallingdal to Stavanger—no doubt because of their inhabitants being 'colonists' from Vestlandet who spoke West Country dialects. Peder Clausson (*ca.* 1600) described the bishop's route from Eidfjord, at the head of Hardangerfjord, and up the stepped hair-pin bends (124 of them) of Maabøgaldene to Hardangervidden. He wrote that 'cold-harbours' were erected along the track across the mountains, one being named 'Biskopsbod.' It was forbidden to risk life on those mountain tracks between 24th August and 3rd May.

In addition to the three English bishops already mentioned, there were some English canons and two priests in the diocese. The latter were William of York and Thorberg of Hertford—both *ca.* 1300—but connexions with the English Church were intimate at all times.

A 'lagting' (law-thing) was established in Stavanger during the Black Death, and assembled regularly after 1351; it was held at Skagen gaard.

Although German craftsmen were permitted to settle down in Stavanger without let or hindrance, the market for their handiwork was too limited to attract them until German merchants took over most of the trade soon after 1400. This expanded so rapidly that a 'town charter' was granted in 1425.

Very little is known about the economic life of Stavanger in early days, but times were good in the twelfth century when export of corn from Jæren and Ryfylke flourished. The bishops monopolized big business before the Black Death, running their 'buses' to King's Lynn, Hull and Ravensworth (opposite Grimsby); fish and codliver oil were exchanged for textiles. Gaute Isakssøn ran ships to England, and in 1303 'Isaksbusser' from Talgje were bringing as cargoes malt, silks, saffron and ginger for Bergen merchants. Shortly after that date the Hansa took that trade away from Rogaland.

Little or nothing is known of the inner life of Stavanger during the seventeenth and eighteenth centuries, except what can be gleaned from the ancient court and borough protocols. In them of course only the seamy side of life appears—murders, witch-hunts and petty quarrels.

During the seventeenth century there were a number of outstanding artists and craftsmen who adorned many of the rural churches. *Peter Reimers*, a German-born painter, is looked upon as the pioneer of the rich ecclesiastical renaissance art around Stavanger. His best work is the reredos in Egersund church: he also painted portraits. *Godtfred Hendtzchel* of Silesia was a spirited painter of religious pictures, and left much behind him that has survived. In the latter half of the seventeenth century the outstanding wood carver *Anders Smith*, an immigrant Scot, came to Stavanger via Bergen. He took citizenship in the former town and his descendants are living there today. His carved pulpit in the cathedral is the finest piece of baroque work in Norway.

After the Reformation the *cathedral* decayed in like manner to the town. That was, however, due to neither demolition—as in the case of Bergen—nor wilful destruction during Swedish invasion, as was the fate of Hamar. After careful modern restorations, St. Svithun stands today as the best-preserved mediæval cathedral in Norway.

The old *Bishop's Palace* was later the residence of the 'amtmann,' but early in the nineteenth century it was acquired by the *Kielland* family. In 1825 it became the Secondary School which it still is. Only the cellars remain of the mediæval palace, the present building being from 1759.

Stavanger lost its 'town charter' in 1686, when it reverted to the status of a mere 'ladested'—but was regranted its privileges in 1690. There were many difficulties to contend with after those two catastrophes, and its population was still no more than 2,200 in 1825. (It is now over 50,000.) Later a thriving export trade sprang up when England adopted a free trade policy, and neutrality in the Crimean War and American Civil War brought much wealth to the city.

The old mansion of *Ledaal*—built 1799–1803 by Gabriel S. Kielland as the country seat of his family—was adapted in 1949 as the Royal residence. The first Kielland came out of Sogndal in Dalane (1751) and founded the firm which was pre-eminent in Stavanger through many decades. Its fortunes were amassed under neutrality around 1800, and it succeeded in surviving the long and disastrous slump that followed the war against England. It was wound up in 1853. *Alexander Kielland* lived at the old mansion of Ledaal: in his novels which are now classics, he has portrayed life in Stavanger from late in the 1700's to *ca.* 1875.

Disaster struck Stavanger in the 1880's when the herring 'turned their dainty noses' further north, and at the same time as sailing ships were outmoded. Banks failed, and one firm followed another into bankruptcy.

The first canning factory was opened in 1873, and six years later the *brisling*—a small sprat whose habitat is the fjords of Ryfylke during the months of June and July—became the most important raw material for canning. Lobsters, spring herring, kippers, as also plums and pears from the orchards of Ryfylke, are other raw materials which find their way into the Stavanger canning factories. The name of *Bjelland* is synonymous with canning—and from some fifty factories in the town, canned products to the value of millions of pounds are consumed in countless homes all over the world. The town which used to be nicknamed *Kielland's* is now the city of *Bjelland*.

Stavanger is also celebrated as the pioneer city in the temperance and missionary movements—the former in 1859, the latter in 1842. A college for missionaries functions here.

The *See of Stavanger* was transferred to Kristiansand in 1684, and the town itself burnt almost to the ground some six months later. Not until 1925 was the ancient bishopric of Stavanger re-established, and its throne is now back in its glorious cathedral.

Ryfylke

Some 17 km. north of Stavanger lies the island of *Utstein*, where Harald Fairhair had a 'kongsgaard,' and Tjorbjørn Hornklove wrote a poem in praise of the victor of Hafrsfjord—'austmenneses king who lives at Utstein.'

It was in the waters just south of Utstein that Erling Skjalgssón was surprised by Olav the Saint—and there 'rygjakongen' met his death. After the abbey was built (*ca.* 1250) it was known as 'Klosterøy,' but records are meagre and it has no consecutive history. Such of its story in mediæval times as has been preserved has already been referred to in this volume (see p. 197).

Utstein is the best preserved abbey in all Norway. Like Avaldsnes church and Stavanger chancel its style is 'Early English.' The nave is in ruins and roofless, but the chancel is used as the island's parish church. A stone well survives from earliest days.

After the Reformation the abbey estate passed through the ownership of many Danish nobles until bought by the wealthy customs controller Johan Garmann (1675–1730)—a grandson of the first of that name who migrated from Haderslev to new-born Christiania in 1628 and made a fortune there. Some of the property remains with his descendants to this very day. The abbey itself—with garden and a stretch of shore—is now in public ownership: there are yet some flowering exotic plants, which must have been introduced by the monks of old. It lies snug and idyllic on the shore of a sheltered bay, and breathes whispers of many an echo from days long gone by—the more so since descendants of the turtle-doves brought by the monks from overseas still fill the air with their billing and cooing.

Farthest out to sea lies the island group of *Kvitesøy*. Its tiny church of St. Clement, only forty feet in length, was built early in twelfth century. Here in 1208 was held that meeting between 'bagler' and 'birchlegs' which closed the worst phase of the disastrous Civil War (see p. 196). The waters round the island have for long been frequented by lobsters, and now fully half of all that are canned in Stavanger come from Kvitesøy's great 'Lobster park'—150 feet by 50 feet with a depth of 5 feet—which can hold up to 40,000 at any one time. The close-season lasts four months—July to November.

Aamøy must surely have been a sacred spot to prehistoric man, since here was cut on the rocks the largest sketch of a ship in all Scandinavia—20 feet in length.

Rennesøy boasts the venerable Norman church of *Sørbø*, probably built by Bishop Reinald (see p. 192).

Talgje (Tolga-Talgøy) island was the home of the mighty Baron Gaut, who was a member of the Council of Regency for Erik II (*ca.* 1280). This property later came to Olav Nilssøn, that old pirate who together with his wife harassed the Hansa (see p. 207). Talgje church—a beautiful small Norman building (*ca.* 1150)—has recently been restored.

Finnøy lies immediately to the north of Talgje. On it stood the estate of *Hestbø*, where the great Ogmundssøn family had their seat during the fourteenth century (see p. 202). Hestby church, being Gothic, is of course of later date than Sørbø or Talgje: in its rectory Niels Henrik *Abel*—the great mathematician—saw the light in 1802.

The large island of *Ombo* has given its name to a famous hybrid plum, which finds its way hence in large quantities to the canning factories of Stavanger.

At *Aardal* on the mainland stands a very old 'stave church'—

possibly sections are previous to 1600. The reredos is a masterpiece of renaissance wood-carving by Godtfred Hendtzchell.

Nedstrand is an ancient trading place where Dutch and Scottish skippers came to fetch timber from the Ryfylke oak forests throughout the sixteenth and seventeenth centuries. To ensure that the Treasury extracted its dues from this flourishing trade, the 'Ryfylke Customs House' functioned here for some fifty years (1637–87). After the forests had been denuded a lively trade began in fresh lobsters, and 'hummerbusser' (lobster-boats) from Holland and Scotland frequented the port. Many Scots settled down, whose descendants live on at Nedstrand today.

History at the great port of *Sauda* is purely contemporary.

Haugaland

The city of *Haugesund* lies some 10 km. south of the border between Rogaland and Hordaland which meet at *Ryvarden*—anciently the northern coastal limit of the tribal territory of the 'ryger.' Haugesund shot up in the nineteenth century, but although it has no ancient history as a town it is surrounded with traditions that are among the most precious in the story of Norway. The prosperity of Haugesund comes entirely from herring; its historical masterpiece, however, lies 2 km. to the north of the town at 'Harald's Monument' (see p. 184).

There are few districts in Norway so filled with national traditions as the island of *Karm* (Karmøy), with its narrow strait *Karmsund* which separates it from the mainland. Whosoever had control of Karmsund was master of all communications with West and North Norway. King Harald Fairhair realized this fact and made his headquarters at *Avaldsnes* (see p. 183).

On the island of Karm some 15 km. south of Avaldsnes stands the farm of Stangeland, where around 1700 lived *Thormod Torfæus*. He was the first modern student of the sagas. An Icelander himself he was born on a small island off Reykjavik in 1636, took his degree in theology at Copenhagen, married Anna Stangeland—widow of the bailiff of Utstein—and acquired through her inheritance the farm of her own name. There he lived until his death in 1719 at the age of eighty-three. He borrowed several ancient saga manuscripts from Copenhagen and transcribed them at his quiet home of Stangeland. Then he named them after the peculiarities of their external appearance, viz.: Fagrskinna, Morkinskinna, Hrokkenskinna and Jofrskinna —names which have been retained and are world-famous among saga readers. In 1682 he was appointed 'historiographer' for Norway: he has been styled 'Norway's first State Antiquary.' Torfæus wrote a lengthy 'History of Norway,' which proved of great value to later historians.

In the summer of 1704, the absolute monarch Frederik IV accompanied by a distinguished following, paid Torfæus a visit. He lies buried in Avaldsnes church, and on the third centenary of his birth (May 1936) celebrations in the grand manner were held here and a portrait bust unveiled in the public gardens of *Kopervik* —a large portion of which town stands on the estate of Stangeland.

It was into Kopervik that a Hansa captain piloted Earl Bothwell (1567), where he was seized by a Danish warship and taken to Bergen to begin his long imprisonment which ended in death in Denmark.

At *Skudesnes* on the southern tip of Karmøy a unique industry flourished after the 1880's—the manufacture of 'foghorns.'

Far out in the ocean lies the lonely island of *Utsira*, much frequented by migratory birds.

Jæren

The praises of the plains of Jæren have been sung divinely by two of its natives—*Arne Garborg* and *Alexander Kielland*. No corner of Norway has yielded so many finds from pre-historic times—indeed it resembles Denmark in that respect as well as in its dearth of hills and forests.

Sola was the home of *Erling Skjalgssón* (*ca.* 1020), who was one of the earliest agriculturalists in Jæren (see p. 186). His 'hall' stood on a hill where later the church was built, whose ruins from the twelfth century can still be seen. Close by—and in stark contrast—is the magnificent aerodrome of Sola, the finest in all Scandinavia.

At *Viste*, some 10 km. north-west of Stavanger, is the Stone Age 'munition factory' of Svarthaala—now occupied by an hotel.

Dalane

Peder Clausson Friis—the priest of Audnedal—wrote (*ca.* 1600): 'Dalane is a land created by a wrathful God.'

Egersund church, originally from 1600 but rebuilt later, is a lovely structure which has internal decorations by the great painter Peter Reimers—profits from herring provided the funds for its restoration.

INDEX

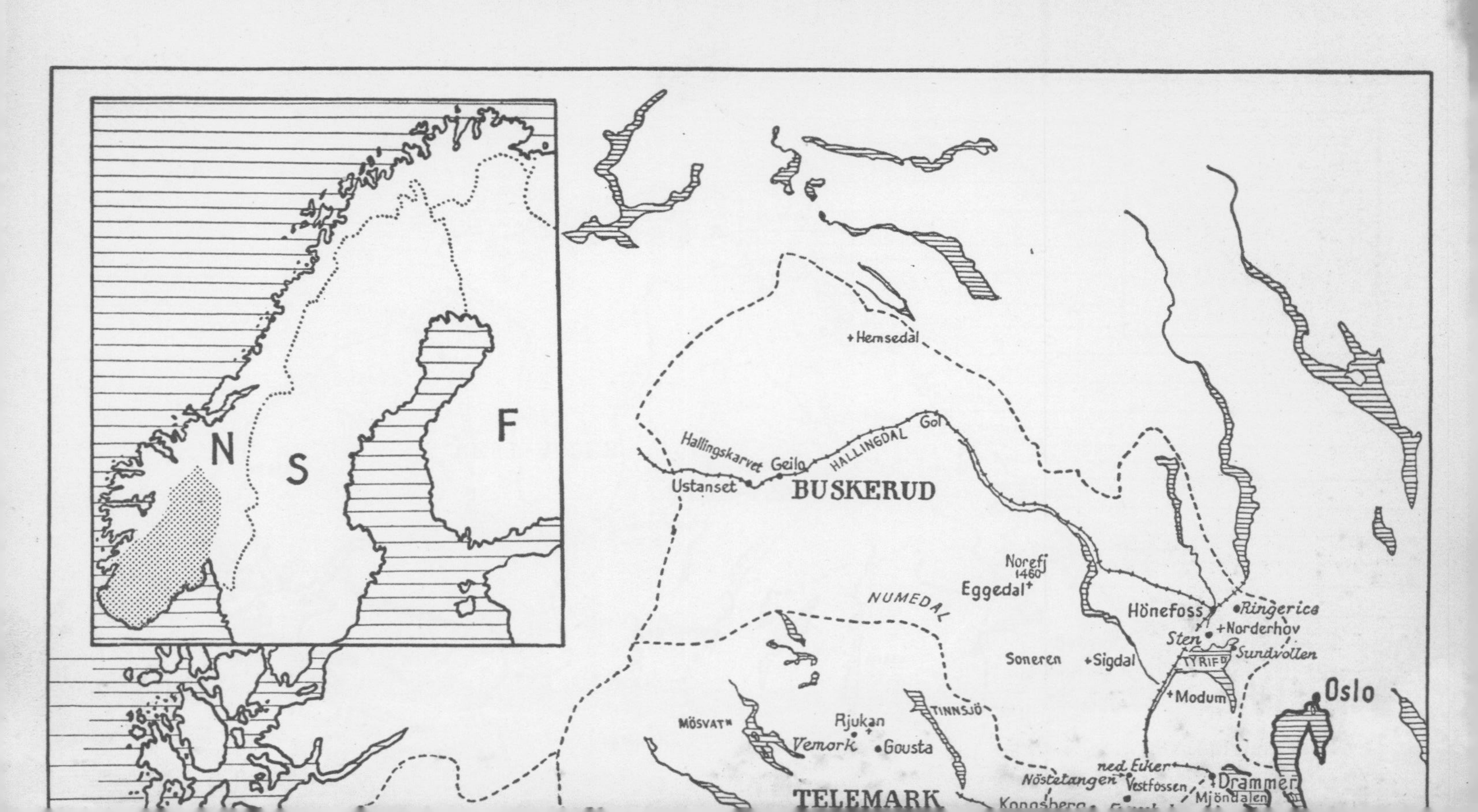
N
S
F
+Hemsedal
Hallingskarvet
Geilo
HALLINGDAL
Gol
Ustanset
BUSKERUD
Norefj
1460
Eggedal+
NUMEDAL
Hönefoss
Ringerice
+Norderhov
Sten
Sundvollen
TYRIF
Soneren
+Sigdal
+Modum
Oslo
MÖSVATN
Rjukan
Vemork
Gousta
TINNSJÖ
ned Eiker
Nöstetangen
Vestfossen
Drammen
Mjöndalen
TELEMARK